English for Academic Study:

Reading

Teacher's Book

John Slaght and Paddy Harben

University of
Reading

ALS
Centre for
Applied Language Studies

Garnet
EDUCATION

Credits

Published by
Garnet Publishing Ltd.
8 Southern Court
South Street
Reading RG1 4QS, UK

First published 2004
Reprinted with corrections 2004
Second edition published 2006
Reprinted 2008
Fully revised 2009
Reprinted 2009

ISBN: 978 1 85964 501 7

British Cataloguing-in-Publication Data
A catalogue record for this book is available from
the British Library.

Production
Project manager: Simone Davies
Project consultant: Rod Webb
Editorial team: Penny Analytis, Simone Davies,
                                    Chris Gough, Fiona McGarry,
                                    Nicky Platt
Design and layout: Mike Hinks

Every effort has been made to trace copyright holders
and we apologise in advance for any unintentional
omissions. We will be happy to insert the appropriate
acknowledgements in any subsequent editions.

Printed and bound
In Lebanon by International Press

Contents

Acknowledgements

The Reading course has been developed to dovetail with the Writing course produced by CALS colleague, Anne Pallant. Anne has played a major role in reviewing material at every stage of development and helping refine the rationale behind the reading into writing approach.

Further significant cooperation in reviewing and editing the materials has come from present and former colleagues at CALS, particularly Ros Richards, Joan McCormack, Colin Campbell, Paul Stocks, Heather Bagley and Sarah Brewer.

In the production of the pilot editions, Paul Thompson contributed considerable IT support and Jill Riley showed great patience and good humour in her painstaking editing and typing.

Pre-sessional teachers from 2000–2005 gave invaluable feedback during trialling of the texts, tasks and teacher's notes.

Many thanks to all the above and also to the many hundreds of students who have already worked with pilot editions of these materials.

A big apology to anyone I have omitted from this list.

John Slaght, Author, April 2009,
Centre for Applied Language Studies,
University of Reading, UK

Book map

Topic	Skills focus
† Economics focus: On the move	Deciding if a text is useful: predicting content
	Word building from a text
	Identifying the organization of a text: analyzing a text to establish the purpose
	Writing a summary of part of the text: complete a gap-fill model
	Dealing with unknown vocabulary: identifying word classes and relative importance of lexis
	Evaluating the level of content: identifying writer's attitude from a range of options
	Reading for a purpose: identifying whether a text is suitable for the reader's purpose
	Reviewing reading styles: reflecting on activities of the unit
1 The influence of class size on academic achievement	Predicting text content: reflecting on personal experience
	Reading for a purpose: predicting content
	Reading selectively: identifying whether a text contains useful information
	Identifying the writer's purpose
	Understanding referencing in texts
A case study: Shining star	Reading a text for closer understanding (1): activities to encourage close reading
The Asian paradox: Huge class sizes, high scores	Reading a text for closer understanding (2): activities to promote close reading
	Thinking critically about the text: reflect on outcome of reading the three texts
	Making use of the text: complete a written assignment
2 Interaction between nature and nurture	Accessing background knowledge: predicting content based on personal experience
	Vocabulary development
	Reading for general understanding: skim read to answer global questions
	Developing further understanding
	Understanding the main argument: identify the best summary
	Note-taking from the text: summarizing specific aspects of the text
	Developing understanding of the text: understanding sequences of events
	Working with words from the text: classify words and discuss their relationships
Capacities of the newborn	Pre-reading discussion
	Inferring meaning from the text
	Summarizing information from the text (1)
	Summarizing information from the text (2)
Hearing, taste and smell	Using background knowledge
	Reading for a purpose and creating a summary
3 Acid rain in Norway	Raising text awareness: activities to elicit personal experience of topic
	Taking information from displayed information: using headings, illustrations, etc.
	Writing a global summary: compare individual work with model summary
Skylarks in decline	More global summary practice: compare individual work with model summary

Topic	Skills focus

4 • Making sense of experience

- Statistics in practice: awareness raising about the topic
- Identifying main and supporting points: read and compare answers
- Continuing to identify main and minor points: read and compare answers
- Summarizing key points (1): complete a gap-fill model
- Summarizing key points (2): complete a gap-fill model

• What is statistics?
- Concentrating on the main points: read and write main points

• Descriptive and inferential statistics
- Note-taking practice: take notes or annotate text in preparation for writing
- Recalling information from the text: write a short summary

5 • Extra-textual information

- Overviewing the text: using extra-textual information and the text introduction
- Writing into reading: compare own notes with information from the text

• Common questions about climate change
- Identifying topic sentences
- Understanding the general meaning of a text: develop understanding of text organization as a means of extracting an overview
- Topic sentences and supporting sentences: read and identify main points and supporting details
- Recalling the text: summarize in writing

• Are human activities contributing to climate change?
- Identifying relevant information in a text: find key points and evaluate relevance of text
- Detailed reading: read and complete a summary
- Recalling the text from memory: write notes from memory

• What human activities contribute to climate change
- Making use of figures and tables: relate display information to sections of the text
- Reading displayed information: relate display information to sections
- Inferring meaning from a text: infer meaning and include in a summary
- Making use of a text: prepare oral presentation or written assignment

6 • Introduction

- Pre-reading discussion
- Checking predictions

• The shrinking planet
- Thinking about the topic
- Recalling the text from memory
- Checking the text for details
- Making use of the text content
- Reading for a purpose

• Economic globalization
- Asking questions about the text
- Identifying key information in the text
- Preparing to complete the Focus task

• Community & conflict
- Thinking about the topic

• The sharing of sovereignty
- Developing understanding of the text

• Converging or diverging?
- Identifying relevant information for the Focus task
- Completing an assignment

7 • The new linguistic order

- Deciding how to read a text
- Reading an introductory case study
- Understanding subject-specific vocabulary
- Predicting content to help understanding
- Selecting relevant information from the text
- Fulfilling your reading purpose

Introduction

In this course students will be working on four main aspects of academic reading:
- reading for a specific academic purpose;
- working on effective reading strategies;
- detailed comprehension of sentences and paragraphs;
- text analysis.

1 Principles and approach

1.1 Towards an appropriate EAP reading methodology

The *middle-way approach* to teaching reading, intended for use with the following materials, is based on practical rather than theoretical considerations. The *middle-way approach* to developing academic reading competence is so called because it involves applying aspects of the *strategies approach* to reading to the *task-based approach* and providing scaffolding by means of comprehension questions, vocabulary work, text analysis tasks, etc., if and when required. Aspects of both the *strategies* and *task-based approaches* to reading are discussed below.

1.2 The *strategies approach* to teaching reading

Reading strategies can be viewed as techniques that are consciously applied in the reading of a text (this excludes automatic/subconscious activity such as word recognition and syntactic processing in efficient readers). It is claimed that effective readers have a range of effective strategies at their disposal. Weir & Urquhart (1998, pp. 94-105) suggest the following reading strategies as being key for academic study:

- *Skimming*: reading quickly and selectively for the main ideas (reading for gist). Typically, most of the text is ignored.
- *Scanning*: reading quickly and selectively in order to locate *words* which have particular importance for the reader (or other symbols, such as figures), i.e., the reader knows the form of words s/he is looking for in advance. This is analogous to word-processing, when you tell the program to search a document for a particular word or phrase. Typically, almost all of the text is ignored. The process involves finding an *exact match* between what the reader is looking for and what is in the text.
- *Search reading*: reading quickly and selectively in order to locate ideas which have particular importance for the reader. This is different from scanning because the form of words is not known in advance, so direct matching is not possible. There is an *inexact match*.
- *Careful reading*: non-selective reading in which the reader reads every word in the text in order to comprehend the writer's meaning in the way the writer encoded it.
- *Browsing*: According to Kintsch & Van Dijk (1978), this occurs where 'people read loosely structured texts with no clear goals in mind. The outcome of such comprehension processes, as far as the resulting macrostructure is concerned, is indeterminate.' Weir & Urquhart claim that browsing does not have to just involve loosely structured texts; virtually any text of reasonable length can be browsed.

The *strategies approach* assumes that, since reading can be improved via training and practice in the use of strategies, reading classes should focus on the development of competence in using a range of strategies.

There are certain positive features of the strategies approach. For example:
- It can lead to the successful use of individual aspects of the approach and therefore to more efficient reading.
- Strategy use does improve with training.
- Strategies may develop into skills (eventually used unconsciously).
- Both students and teachers are comfortable with strategy training because it involves something tangible and clear-cut to 'learn' or 'teach'.

However, there are also some aspects of the strategies approach which would not appear to be appropriate to the needs of the student about to embark on a course of academic studies at university level. For example:
- The mechanical application of strategies is not a guarantee of successful reading. After training, strategies may be used mechanically, even when they are not appropriate; or strategies may not be used, although appropriate, because the reader fails to detect the environment in which to apply them.
- The approach may be deemed to be 'artificially' successful, for instance, in an EAP language-testing situation, where the reader might be instructed to match headings from a headings bank to selected paragraphs in a text (IELTS), or to summarize the accompanying text globally. However, this approach does not always appear to mirror real-life situations.
- Although there is plenty of empirical evidence that natural reading in many situations is strategic, it is also clear that such strategy use is highly flexible and complex (Pressley & Afflerbach, 1995). Reading is an idiosyncratic process and the strategies approach does not allow for the unpredictability of individual acts of reading. Strategy training makes the reader better at employing the strategy when prompted to do so, but does not necessarily ensure that such strategies are used appropriately in autonomous reading situations.
- Kern (1997) warns that the 'implicit universality' in the propositions involved in the strategies approach may be problematic because the propositions are so generalized. He suggests that what is 'useful' for comprehension is far from universal or generic, and there is 'no absolute right time, place, or manner of using strategies for all readers for a given text and context.' He concludes that, although comprehension depends on an effective mix of top-down and bottom-up processing, this mix cannot be prescribed to developing readers. This is because natural text processing is dependent on a number of reader, textual and contextual variables, and so teaching lists of strategies simply will not do.

1.3 The *task-based approach* to teaching reading

This approach suggests that classroom reading tasks should mirror authentic reading demands and purposes outside the classroom. It also suggests that in natural reading situations, effective readers are motivated by a desire to acquire knowledge about a topic that is addressed in the text they are reading. This gives them a clear purpose for reading that helps them to decide how to tackle the text. This purpose can be seen as a task, which is an important influence on how readers approach the text.

Academic reading involves getting information in order to fulfil an academic purpose, for example:
- To complete an assignment on a specific question, for which synthesizing information from various sources is necessary, e.g., to submit an essay or give a spoken presentation.
- To develop an introductory overview of a new topic to help follow a series of lectures on that topic.
- To develop and deepen knowledge of a topic. This could involve deliberate storage of information for later use, e.g., note-taking for future exam revision. Alternatively the focus could be on reading and *thinking* in order to achieve a more developed understanding held in the mind, i.e., in long-term memory.

The *task-based approach* implies a rejection of strategy training. Reading competence cannot be improved simply by training in specific strategies. This is because such an approach ignores the role that real-life reading purposes have on influencing which strategies a given reader will find appropriate when dealing with a specific text. Furthermore, different texts pose different kinds of problems for readers from different language and cultural backgrounds, while individual differences in prior knowledge, motivation and reading purpose also contribute to the way texts are tackled. Reading instruction should therefore be context-sensitive, and grounded in specific texts and reading tasks.

In the strategies model, the information required from the text is decided by the strategy selected. In the task-based model, the information required is directly specified by the reader's purpose for reading, to which any strategy is subservient. In such an approach, the readers/students are given an academic task parallel to a natural academic task involving reading. Typically, they will be given:
- a text or texts concerning a specific topic;
- a task to complete concerning that topic.

For example, they may be given a text or a collection of texts and asked to answer a question which requires synthesizing various ideas in the text(s), which functions as a 'Focus task' for their reading. In principle, the nature of the task directs the use the reader makes of the text(s), the reading process, and consequently shapes the final product of the reader's efforts.

In the task-based approach, the processes and strategies occurring are dependent on the task, text and reader variables mentioned by Kern (above), and the reader has to make autonomous decisions about what is needed from the text. The end product, the completed 'Focus task', can be compared with a model, and evaluative decisions can be made by the reader about the degree of success that has been achieved.

There are certain positive features of the task-based approach relevant to the needs of the EAP reader about to begin an academic course. For example:
- The reading conditions mirror those of natural academic reading. In particular, the purpose for reading is the pursuit of relevant information to complete an academic task. The students are 'reading to learn, not learning to read' (Shih, 1992).
- The use of strategies is determined by the reader.

However, there are also negative features implicit in the teaching of the task-based approach. For example:
- It is a deep-end approach, which raises important questions if students struggle to use it effectively.
  - What happens if the reader is unable to fulfil the task successfully? Should the teacher intervene? If so, how?
  - How does failure to complete the task improve a student's reading?
  - How can students who fail to complete the task stay motivated to improve?
- The teacher's role is also problematic. If it is restricted to setting the Focus task and evaluating the product, both students and teachers may ask, 'Where is the *teaching* in all this?'

1.4 A proposed *middle-way* approach

With this approach, the reader is encouraged to bridge the gap between the two previously mentioned approaches in the following ways:
- **a)** Students are encouraged to explore/discuss strategy use in different situations. The key to doing this successfully is self-monitoring.
- **b)** The task provides a purpose for reading, but the student can monitor the reading at three stages: pre-reading, while reading and post-reading.

1.4.1 Pre-reading: *How am I going to carry out this task?*

The reader can be encouraged to make decisions about how to carry out the task in relation to the purpose for reading, the time available for reading and the prior knowledge s/he has (both conceptual and linguistical). For example, in Unit 4, *Statistics without tears*, the focus is on summarizing a section of the text. During the course of the unit, the students discuss the appropriate level of detail for a summary: whether it is always the same or if it depends on certain factors; if so, what they are and how they determine the level of detail required, etc.

Unit 3a, *The environment today*, suggests a different approach, in which the students are encouraged to access their *prior knowledge* by making use of the title and other overt information, such as tables and figures. It also suggests that focusing on certain key words displayed in the heading, subheadings and captions in the text, helps the reader access the content 'quickly and efficiently'. Students are encouraged to consider ways of gaining a quick global summary of the text, and are then invited to discuss other ways of rapidly accessing information for global comprehension. These can be compared with a 'master checklist' of notes for students to compare with their own notes (provided in the Teacher's Book as photocopiable handouts: note that all the photocopiable materials in this book are also available as downloadable files in the teacher's section of the EAS website – www.englishforacademicstudy.com). The students are thus encouraged to devise whatever strategies occur to them and add them to the master list, if appropriate. The aim is to discourage the mechanical application of any particular strategy, and to develop a strategy that suits the needs of the individual reader and the nature of the individual text. Imposing a strict time limit for finding information and summarizing introduces further authentic variables.

1.4.2 While reading: *How successfully am I carrying out the reading in relation to the task I am performing?*

There are questions at the end of each section of *Statistics without tears* to help students monitor their understanding of the text. Thus, they can check whether they have come to the right conclusions because the next section provides the answers within the body of the text. If the students do not fully understand each section, their summaries will probably be inaccurate.

Throughout the course, students should be encouraged to keep asking questions of the text while they are reading. This will help them make decisions about how to tackle the text. Similarly, a photocopiable 'official checklist' is included in certain units of the Teacher's Book as photocopiable handouts so students can check at various stages of their reading whether their notes relate appropriately to the demands of the Focus task. Thus, the student is monitoring the ongoing product of her/his reading, which should make the reading purposeful and, hopefully, motivating.

1.4.3 Post-reading: *How did I carry out the task? Do I need to rethink my approach to the text in order to complete the Focus task more successfully?*

In Unit 3a, students are given a model summary to compare with their own, a 'tick box' activity to indicate the level of success they have noted, and a further exercise to encourage them to think about if and why they had problems. A second text for global comprehension, *Skylarks in decline*, is provided, which is significantly different in outlay and content from the first, e.g., only the heading and subheadings and one figure provide 'display' clues about content. There is no introduction with this text, simply a task. However, the same time limits are imposed with the aim that once the summary task has been completed, the students autonomously decide how effective their strategy for reading this text and completing the task has been in comparison with (a) a model summary, and (b) the previous summary they completed for *Acid rain in Norway*. Students can then decide whether both texts can be successfully tackled in the same way or whether different strategies need to be applied. In this way, students are given the opportunity to carry out an identical task with very different texts and to 'sample' a range of possible strategies that they can employ independently.

1.4.4 Comprehension work

It is clearly important that the student should be successful in the 'while reading' stage; it is this stage that will provide feedback on how s/he is progressing as well as practice in developing new skills. The approach therefore makes use of comprehension work as a form of scaffolding. Thus, if the text is too difficult for students successfully to complete the proposed product autonomously, they can do so with the teacher's guidance. Basically, the purpose of the comprehension questions is to provide potential products that the students need along the way for Focus task completion.

There are a number of practical ways in which comprehension questions can be used. In order for the materials to be adapted to the level and needs of the students, the materials have been divided into three separate books: (a) a Source Book; (b) a Course Book; and (c) a Teacher's Book. The majority of the comprehension tasks intended for scaffolding are contained only in the Teacher's Book; only if individual students, or occasionally the whole class, are experiencing difficulties should they be provided. These comprehension-scaffolding tasks are located on individual pages in the Teacher's Book for ease of photocopying, so they can be prepared as handouts or as overhead transparencies (OHTs).

Paragraph-matching exercises are particularly useful. In Unit 7, *The new linguistic order*, the fairly lengthy text is divided up into three appropriate sections, and at the end of each section a paragraph summary-matching task is provided. Vocabulary-matching tasks are also provided. Essentially, any of a wide range of traditional comprehension question formats can be successfully used, e.g., multiple-choice, true/false, SAQs, jigsaw and matching activities.

There are two key conditions for using comprehension questions in the middle-way approach. Firstly, such questions should be seen as scaffolding, to be used only when required, in order that the reader should achieve her/his reading purpose. Secondly, they may be used as an independent syllabus strand, to focus on core comprehension difficulties.

The middle-way approach to EAP reading is designed to incorporate elements of both the strategies approach and the task-based approach to reading. At the same time, it is intended to encourage reader autonomy through self-monitoring at the pre-, while- and post-reading stages. Students are encouraged to interact with the text by monitoring their comprehension at all stages of reading, and models are provided for comparison at all three of these reading stages. The models are introduced and used either as master checklists or summaries. Other forms of scaffolding are introduced depending on the needs of the students. Such scaffolding includes typical comprehension task formats as well as vocabulary work. Through a range of materials, students are encouraged to 'sample' strategies and make personal decisions about if and when to use them.

Reading for a purpose is key to the middle-way approach, as it is with the task-based approach. It is important to persuade students to adopt an approach to developing reading competence which is particularly appropriate to the demands of academic reading at tertiary level.

2 Using *EAS Reading*

2.1 Developing referencing skills using the *Reading & Writing Source Book*

Students using these *Reading* materials in conjunction with the *Writing* book (Pallant 2004) will be expected either to quote directly, or to summarize or paraphrase sections of the various texts in order to fulfil their reading purpose.

In the context of these materials, summarizing is understood as:

- *reducing the whole or part of the text without changing the ideas or organization of the original text.*

Paraphrasing is understood as:

- *using the ideas of an original source in order to support or refute an argument, opinion or idea; this may involve a degree of 'interpretation' of the original text.*

It is clearly necessary for students to develop the skills for referencing in an appropriately academic style. These skills can be developed in three ways: recognizing different styles of referencing, acknowledging sources and evaluating sources.

2.1.1 Recognizing different styles of referencing

Students need to recognize that different sources will be referenced in different ways. The Source Book in this series contains text types from a range of sources, for example:

- serious magazine articles intended for the general reading public or for educational purposes such as from *The Economist*, *Scientific American* or *Understanding Global Issues*;
- texts taken from more academic sources such as Atkinson R.L. et al.'s *Hilgard's introduction to psychology*, and from an academic journal *Foreign Policy*, or from a book described as a 'primer for non-mathematicians', Derek Rowntree's *Statistics without tears*.

Exposure to and general discussion comparing the style, content and intended readership is an important study skill, which should not be neglected in the development of academic reading proficiency.

It is important that the difference in text styles is regularly pointed out to students so that, for example, in Unit 2, *Early human development*, there are a range of examples of internal referencing (see page 13, right-hand column). In Unit 5, *Human activity and climate change*, however, the original source is a brochure which was compiled at the behest of the UN Environment Programme: World Meteorological Organization and the text has been compiled by a number of academics. As a result, no exact authorship is attributed to any specific contributor in the original document. In such a case, when students wish to quote or paraphrase from the text, it would be best for them to indicate authorship as Hamburg et al. (updated 2004*) because Steven Hamburg is mentioned first in the alphabetically-arranged list of contributors. It is important for students to appreciate that the origin of this source is very different from other texts in the same Source Book.

*Since the original completion of the source materials, two of the texts have become available online. These are Human activity and climate change *and* The new linguistic order. *They can be viewed at http://www.gcrio.org/ipcc/qa/contributors.html (click on 'Common Questions' about Climate Change) and http://www.uoc.edu/humfil/articles/eng/fishman/fishman.html respectively. Students could be encouraged to visit these sites and, in fact, to reference them accordingly in their work.*

2.1.2 Acknowledging sources

Students need to appreciate the importance of acknowledging their sources. They should be made aware that *not* referencing amounts to theft of intellectual property and can have serious repercussions. At the same time they need to realize that by quoting and/or acknowledging their sources, writers actually add more weight to their arguments and ideas.

2.1.3 Evaluating sources

Students clearly need to assess the currency of any text they use to fulfil their reading purpose and the credentials of the authors. As much guidance as possible is provided in the Source Book for this purpose (see for examples the bibliographical information supplied about the authors of *Acid rain* or *Skylarks in decline*), and there is ample opportunity to explore the credentials and currency of the authors by going beyond the Source Book. For example, although the article

Economics focus: On the move is not strictly academic, the text *International Migration & The Integration of Labour* (Chiswick & Hatton 2002), referred to in *The Economist* article is very much so. In fact, students can be encouraged to verify this for themselves by viewing the abstract for this text by utilizing their university library service's online or hardcopy facilities.

Students need to take into consideration the source of any text they use and the original intended readership. At some stage during the teaching of every unit, this should be a general teaching point. The students should consider the relative academic weight that certain texts may carry in comparison with others in the Source Book. In addition, teachers should draw students' attention to the fact that a range of texts has been used in the materials in order to develop students' exposure to relatively dense and content-packed texts, in preparation for their future academic studies.

2.2 Unit summaries

These provide an opportunity for the students to reflect on what they have done at the end of each unit. You may wish the students to complete the unit summaries in class or in their own time. If they complete them out of class, make sure you find time to discuss what the students have done.

2.3 Other features

2.3.1 Glossary
This contains a useful list of terms that the students will need to know during the course.

2.3.2 Study tips
These contain additional information that can be used by the students as a ready reference to a range of study issues related to the reading skill.

2.3.3 Web resources
There are suggested web resources at the end of each unit. These provide further areas of practice or study on topics or skills related to the unit.

2.4 Routes through the materials

These *EAS Reading* materials can either be used in combination with *Writing* materials published in the same series, or as a stand-alone course. The books are designed for international students of English intending to pursue academic study in an English-speaking environment, whose IELTS level is between 5.0 and 7.5. However, much of the material can be adapted for use with less proficient students studying on extended courses.

One of the key principles underpinning the approach taken to academic reading is the idea that it should be *purposeful*. The type of information required to complete the writing task will determine the type of reading needed to extract the relevant information and ideas from the text. Note that a writing task is indicated in many of the units of the *EAS Reading* materials. However, an extended approach to integrated reading and writing skills can be fully developed through using the *EAS Writing* book.

Students requiring additional help with any issues relating to the use of language should be encouraged to refer to a general grammar reference text, such as Swan, M., & Walter, C. (2009) *The good grammar book*. Oxford: OUP.

A number of routes through the reading materials are suggested on page 15, depending on the length of the intended course and the number of probable teaching hours required to reach the minimum university entrance level. These are based on two 90-minute lessons per week. The amount of work given to students to be completed outside class time will vary. Students with a higher level of English language are expected to cover the units more quickly than lower-level students.

Note: In some cases, the allocation of time will not allow for reading all of the texts in the *Source Book* during class time, and in certain cases, only time for partial reading in class will be possible. By the time students progress to later units they should have developed their reading strategies sufficiently to work on at least some of the texts independently outside class; this should certainly be the case with Unit 6, for example. The ability to work independently by the time students begin their academic studies through the medium of English is an essential goal of any international student.

Note: Non-contact hours = homework and private study related to the materials.

Suggested route for 16-week course

Week	Contact hours	Non-contact hours	Unit
1	3	4	Task intro.
2	3	4	Task intro.
3	3	4	Unit 1
4	3	4	Unit 1
5	3	4	Unit 2
6	3	4	Unit 2
7	3	4	Unit 3
8	3	4	Unit 4
9	3	4	Unit 4
10	3	4	Unit 5
11	3	4	Unit 5
12	3	4	Unit 6*
13	3	4	Unit 6
14	3	4	Unit 6
15	3	4	Unit 7*
16	3	4	Unit 7

*It is intended that students are encouraged to take considerably more responsibility for independent study with Units 6 and 7.

Suggested route for 11-week course

Week	Contact hours	Non-contact hours	Unit
1	1.5	2	Task intro.
1	1.5	2	Unit 1
2	1.5	2	Unit 1
2	1.5	2	Unit 2
3	1.5	4	Unit 2
3	1.5	0	Unit 3
4	3	4	Unit 4
5	3	4	Unit 4
6	3	4	Unit 5
7	3	4	Unit 5
8	3	4	Unit 6
9	3	4	Unit 6
10	1.5	0	Unit 6
10	1.5	4	Unit 7
11	3	4	Unit 7

Suggested route for 8-week course

Week	Contact hours	Non-contact hours	Unit
1	3	4	Task intro.
2	3	4	Unit 1
3	3	4	Unit 2
4	1.5	0	Unit 3
4	1.5	4	Unit 4
5	1.5	0	Unit 4
6	1.5	4	Unit 6
7	3	4	Unit 6
8	3	4	Unit 6*

*It is important that all students work fully on Unit 6, which puts into practice the idea of selective reading for a purpose and the need for students to take responsibility for their own reading needs. On the 8-week course, higher-level groups may progress sufficiently to attempt Unit 7 in Week 8, or go back to Unit 5 for consolidation work.

Suggested route for 5-week course

Week	Contact hours	Non-contact hours	Unit
1	1.5	1	Task intro.
	1.5	3	Unit 1
2	3	0	Unit 2
3	3	4	Unit 4
4	3	4	Unit 6
5	3	4	Unit 6

References

Bamford, J., & Day, R.R. (1998). Teaching reading. *Annual Review of Applied Linguistics*, 124–135.

Hudson, T. (1998). Theoretical perspectives on reading. *Annual Review of Applied Linguistics*, 43–60.

Kern, R.G. (1997). L2 reading strategy training: A critical perspective. *Annual Review of Applied Linguistics*, 103–117.

Kintsch, W., & Van Dijk, T.A. (1978). Towards a model of text comprehension and production. *Psychological Review*, 85, 363–394.

Pressley, M., & Afflerbach, P. (1995). *Verbal Protocols of Reading: The Nature of Constructively Responsive Reading*, Lawrence Erlbaum Associates.

Shih, M. (1992). Beyond comprehension exercises in the ESL academic reading class. *TESOL Quarterly*, 26(2), 289–318.

Slaght, J. (1999). *Academic Reading: A Theoretical Overview*, (unpublished paper), The University of Reading.

Urquhart, S., & Weir, C. (1998). *Reading in a Second Language: Process, Product & Practice*. New York: Longman.

Task introduction

This unit will help students:
- practice and review the reading strategies outlined in the introduction;
- develop strategies for deciding if a text is useful;
- build vocabulary through reading;
- identify a text's organization;
- write a summary as part of understanding key issues.

Text i-1 | Economics focus: On the move

Focus task

Make sure the students fully understand the scenario described in the Focus task. It is essential that the students get the idea of reading for a purpose (even if it is an imaginary one) from the beginning.

Task 1: Deciding if a text is useful

The aim of this task is to encourage students to read selectively in order to achieve their reading purpose. It should also discourage them from laboriously working their way through a text from start to finish.

1.1 Establish with the students their *purpose* in reading the text as described in the Focus task.

Point out the italicized introduction. Tell the students to read the heading and subheadings too. It may be a good idea for students to highlight these in their books.

Answers:
b) an educated general reader*

Possible reasons:
- The source of the text (*The Economist*).
- The type of information (fairly superficial; quite a lot of background information that a specialist would not expect to read; not very technical).
- The style of writing (relatively short sentences; short paragraphs).

*c) and d) are also possible choices, but point out that an Economics student or a historian would probably read a text with more specialist content, unless they wanted a more general introduction to the topic area.

Note: The subheading, which refers to the history of immigration, might encourage students to choose the historian option.

1.2 Refer students to the title and subtitle, and ask them to predict the content from the key words, e.g., *economics*, *history of immigration*, *future*. Also refer them to the introductory and concluding paragraphs.

There are additional important clues from:
- The name of the journal/magazine = *The Economist*.
- The section of the journal = *Finance and Economics*.
- The date of publication.

Also point out the reference at the end of the article to a website (line 218). If the students visit this site they will find it contains a discussion paper on international migration.

From the introductory paragraph, get students to identify the main topic of the article, i.e., lines 5–8; 12–15; 25–29.

Students may be able to identify the historical/chronological order of the information, e.g., lines 3–5 … *the three centuries leading up to the First World War*. This chronological description/analysis runs from line 30 to line 155 (and less obviously through to the end of the text).

1.3 Students can check the accuracy of their predictions as they work through the following tasks (this is an important part of the self-monitoring process which these materials hope to encourage).

Task 2: Word-building from a text

This task has two aims. The first aim is to get students to identify key words in the text, either because they appear in the headings, etc., or because they occur frequently in the main body of the text. The secondary aim is to encourage the recognition of the morphological make-up of words: stems, prefixes and suffixes. The specific aim of Task 2 is to help students analyze the morphological link between words derived from the same stem. It should give students a confidence boost to work out the meaning of some words if they can recognize the stem word.

2.1/2.2 Before students start scanning the text, tell them that when you scan a text you know exactly what you are looking for and tend to ignore everything else in the text. This is similar to looking for someone's name in a telephone directory.

Explain to students that, by recognizing word class, they will be able to see the function, or purpose of words. This in turn will help them to work out meaning and how important the words are to the writer. Often, knowing the meaning of nouns can be more immediately useful than adjectives or adverbs (with adjectives, the key is usually recognizing whether they are positive or negative in meaning).

The *Connected language* column of the table is included to get students thinking in terms of working out meaning from context and also to get them to recognize how words collocate, i.e., occur naturally together in a language.

Possible answers:

Word used	Line number	Word class	Connected language
migration	line 18	noun	to restrict migration
immigrants	lines 55–56	noun	some 8m immigrants
emigration	line 79	noun	a rare case for America of net emigration
migrate	line 145	verb	workers who can migrate

2.3 Point out that there is also an adjective *migrant*, as in *migrant worker*.

You could get students to suggest other examples of how the verb, adjective and noun forms work in context.

Discuss the difference between *emigration* and *immigration*, paying attention to the prefixes:

- *Immigration* is when people come into a country to live and work there.

- *Emigration* is when you leave your own country to live in another one.

Example:

A lot of migrant workers *emigrated* from Britain to the USA. This *migration* of British people occurred particularly at the end of the 19th century. The *immigrants* often first arrived in New York before *migrating* to another part of the United States.

Task 3: Identifying the organization of a text

The aim of this task is to get students to look more carefully at the text once they have grasped some of the main ideas. By looking at the organization of the text, students should get a clear picture of the main ideas and start to identify the supporting ideas.

3.1 Answer:

The most obvious division is the subtitle *Winners and losers*. Prior to this, the text deals with background information on migrationary trends. This section deals with the effects of migration on both the sending and receiving countries.

3.2 The first section of the text provides an introduction and background historical information from the 16th to the 20th centuries, focusing mainly on Europe and the United States. The second part is more analytical in approach.

Answers:
- The main aim is the link between migration and economic factors, e.g., lines 1–15.
- The purpose of paragraphs 2–4 is to trace the history and pattern of migration from Europe to the USA in relation to economic factors.

Ask lower-level students to highlight the various historical stages in the text, using the dates, etc.

3.3 Answer:

The main purpose of the second half of the text is to analyze the effects of migration, i.e., the effects in host countries, and reasons for expansion of migration; explanation of rising incomes in rich and poor countries; differences between previous centuries and the current situation.

It could prove useful to get students to highlight sentences that contain verbs reporting the effects of migration, e.g., line 104 … *The evidence suggests that … receiving countries*; line 152 … *Several studies suggest that …*

Task 4: Writing a summary of part of the text

The purpose of these four exercises is to encourage students to carry out post-reading monitoring of their understanding by making brief notes of what they have understood.

4.2 Answers:
- economic factors
- slaves
- began to migrate/migrated
- the 19th century
- economic depression
- migration

4.4 Answers:
1 Paragraph B
2 Paragraph D
3 Paragraph A

Task 5: Dealing with unknown vocabulary

5.1 Answers depend on students.

5.2 Explain to students that there is no hard and fast way of knowing whether a word is classified as (a), (b) or (c). It will depend very much on their needs. Students can be encouraged to consult the Academic Word List (AWL) or the General Service List (GSL) to see whether it appears that the word is relatively high frequency. The AWL is very familiar to most teachers of English for Academic Purposes and should be made familiar to all international students on pre-sessional courses. The AWL is a list of words which occur with higher frequency, originating from Averil Coxhead of Victoria University, Wellington (NZ). It is based on an analysis of mainly academic source texts; e.g., text books, lab reports and academic journals across most academic disciplines. It comprises 750 head words and 10 sub-lists; Sub-list 1, for example, includes the most frequently occurring words and so on. For further information, please visit http://www.uefap.com/vocab/select/awl.htm. Students can also try Wiktionary to view the words in each of the 10 sub-lists at http://simple.wiktionary.org/wiki/Wiktionary:Academic_word_list.

The GSL, however, lists the 2000 words most frequently occurring in more general, basic English. This can be checked at: http://jbauman.com/gsl.html . Of course, many words such as *area*, *similar*, *create* and *occur* appear in both lists.

Students can also be encouraged to visit appropriate websites to help them make decisions about vocabulary.

5.3 **Answer:**
The world[n] *has experienced*[vb] *a new*[adj] *era of globalization*[n]*, which*[pron] *is*[vb] *much*[adv] *quicker*[adj]*.

5.4 **Answers:**
(Choice of a, b or c depends on students.)

Vocabulary	a	b	c	Word class
makes plain				verb (phrase)
harsh				adjective
indentured*				adjective
slavery				noun
falling				adjective
comparatively				adverb
net				adjective
feasible				adjective
expansionary				adjective

*Check with students whether they have noticed how the word *indentured* is defined in the following sentence (lines 44–48): *This meant that the workers were forced to work for their bosses for a period of time without pay.*

Task 6: Evaluating the level of content

The aim of this task is to encourage critical thinking about the content of the text and aims of the writer.

Encourage students to identify sections of the text that they could use to justify their choice – they can just note line numbers. Remind students of the importance of discussing texts when in an academic environment. Explain that such discussion will help consolidate their understanding of the text and thus is an important pre-, while- and post-reading skill to practise.

Answer:
It seems that in the first part of the text (up to line 100) the writer's main purpose is (a) to inform the reader (to give background information about the link between economic forces and immigration from Europe to America). The second half of the text does appear to give a 'balanced' opinion (d), e.g., lines 104–109. There is also a strong element of sympathy, for example, on humanitarian grounds (lines 176–181) for the less fortunate would-be immigrant. This is reinforced in the conclusion; therefore, the writer seems to be hoping to persuade the reader to accept her/his opinion (b).

Task 7: Reading for a purpose

The aim of this task is to remind students that academic reading is normally carried out for a specific purpose. Elicit that their reading purpose was to have some background knowledge before attending the first lecture about the link between migration and economic forces. There are a number of reasons why the students might feel that the text was either useful or not useful. These are just a few.

It might have been considered useful because:
- the reader had no previous knowledge of this idea;
- the text supplemented previous knowledge;
- it provided the reader with a different point of view.

In each of the above cases, the text will have fulfilled the reader's purpose to a greater or lesser extent.

The text might have been considered not useful because:
- the contents were too simple or too complex;
- the reader wanted more specific information about a particular migratory pattern;
- the writer may have expressed views which the reader disagrees with.

In each of these cases, the reader's purpose will not have been fulfilled.

Task 8: Reviewing reading styles

The purpose of this task is to get students to reflect on the contents of this introductory unit. This should be treated purely as a round-up session and will depend very much on the level of the students. The task should be considered in tandem with the appropriate unit in *EAS Writing*.

8.1 Get students to discuss the questions. This will probably be done most usefully in small groups. Each group can be given one or two of these questions to discuss. This should be followed up with a whole-group discussion directed by the teacher, focusing on all the questions.

8.2 Suggested answers to the questions in Ex 8.1 are given on the next page so that they can either be photocopied and visually displayed as a source of discussion, or used as a checklist.

Task 8

Discussion points

a) Predicting contents

- Brings to mind words and language associated with the topic
- Helps understanding
- Encourages readers to use general background knowledge to improve understanding

b) Reading strategies

- Different ways of reading a text, e.g., skimming, predicting
- Different strategies can be used depending on the text type, how difficult the text is, and why the text is being read

c) Global understanding

- General understanding of the whole text or a selected part of the text
- Global understanding is useful for understanding main ideas or information, understanding the purpose of the text, and recognizing the attitude of the writer
- Global understanding helps the reader decide how important the text is
- Global understanding helps the reader decide whether to read the text again and what reading strategies to use

d) Word-for-word reading

- Demotivating – the reader may lose interest
- Time-consuming
- May lead to unsuccessful reading habits
- Readers may forget their purpose for reading
- May lead to poor understanding

e) Selective reading

- Only part of the text may be useful for the reader's purpose
- Saves time

f) The intended reader

- The style (and register) will vary depending on the intended reader, e.g., formal, neutral or informal, leading to different complexities of sentence construction, vocabulary and general organization
  - An undergraduate textbook will often be less specialized than a journal article or a textbook intended for a postgraduate reader
  - A text intended for general readers may not be useful for the purposes of an academic reader

Photocopiable

1 Academic achievement

This unit will help students:
- use their prior knowledge to help them understand what they are reading;
- practise reading for a specific purpose;
- make decisions about the relevance of a text in terms of reading purpose;
- read selectively in order to use appropriate information from the text.

The topics and texts in this book are designed to encourage students to read for a specific purpose. The most common reading purpose during university study is to complete written assignments. It is for this reason that *EAS Reading* is linked to its companion course *EAS Writing*. Although the students do not have to complete the writing course alongside *EAS Reading*, it is nevertheless useful to read as if they will be going on to do the specified writing tasks.

The Focus task in Unit 1 of *EAS Writing* is to write a second draft of an essay: *What are the aims of academic study and how can they be achieved?* The students are encouraged to make alterations to their first draft based on reading they carry out in this unit of *EAS Reading*. As parts of the reading text in this unit are more relevant to the writing Focus task than others, students are encouraged to read selectively and to make decisions about which areas of the text are relevant to their writing needs.

Students who are not using *EAS Writing* in conjunction with this course should nevertheless feel that they could be carrying out the reading as writing research to help develop a sense of purpose in reading. In this unit students are encouraged to read selectively and to make decisions about which areas of the text are relevant to their real or imaginary writing needs.

In most English-medium universities or colleges, an independent learning style will be expected of students undertaking degree courses. Students should be encouraged to make their own decisions about the contents of this text in terms of the Focus task, i.e., whether:
   a) the whole text is useful for their purpose and therefore requires thorough detailed understanding;
   b) only certain parts of the text are particularly relevant.

The text has been chosen with the view that certain areas are more relevant than others and this will become clear as they do the tasks in the unit. However, the decision about which areas are most relevant should ultimately be left to the student.

Text 1-1   The influence of class size on academic achievement

Task 1: Predicting text content

It is intended that after reading the whole article, students can return to this task and reconsider their initial ratings.

1.3 After working individually and in pairs, encourage students to suggest other factors as a whole class and reach a consensus about how they should be rated in terms of importance.

Other suggested influences:
- The ratio of teachers to students, i.e., class size
- The socio-economic background of the students
- Parental influence
- Discipline at school and at home

- The ethos/reputation of the school/college
- Funding and support, e.g., from governmental or non-governmental sources

Accept or offer up for discussion any further reasonable suggestions.

Task 2: Reading for a purpose

This task is intended to re-emphasize the need to read for a purpose. Get the students to look at the Focus task, *What are the aims of academic study and how can they be achieved?*, and get them to verbalize exactly what they are aiming to do. They may need to simplify the question in their own words in order to understand fully what to do.

2.1 Remind students of the work they did in the introductory unit about looking at the title of a text as well as subtitles, graphics and other meta-textual features (e.g., tables, figures) in order to make decisions about how to read it.

2.2 Answers:
Possible reasons why the text might be considered useful:
- It deals with a factor which might impact on academic achievement – the reduction of class size.
- It seems to weigh up the pros and cons of reducing class size.
- The article refers to studies carried out on the impact of class size on academic achievement in Tennessee, California and Wisconsin.

Possible reasons why the text might not be considered useful:
- It refers to the American school system (but point out that later on in the text, reference is made to other countries).
- It concentrates on school children; relating this to university level might not be considered appropriate.

Task 3: Reading selectively

3.1 Reiterate the strategy of thinking about the content of a text before reading it as a useful way of enhancing understanding. Give students no more than two or three minutes to write down their reasons. Encourage them to write in note form.

3.2 Answers:
a) Yes (lines 73–75)
b) No
c) Yes (lines 77–79; you need to explain *cooperative learning* briefly)
d) Yes (lines 81–82)
e) Yes (lines 91–92)
f) No (this is not mentioned in the text)
g) No (the opposite, in fact; lines 106–115)

3.3 Answer:
anecdotal = subjective; unreliable
As the explanations are *anecdotal*, they are not apparently supported by research findings and are, rather, the subjective views of teachers, parents or other interested people. From an academic point of view, such opinions cannot be taken too seriously because they lack concrete evidence, i.e., are not backed by research data.

3.4 Students should appreciate that this paragraph could contain some very useful information because it is backed by research.

The information that the students might most usefully highlight includes:
- Lines 108–110: '... the improvement in academic performance was negligible';
- Lines 109–115: '... data from ... a series of texts ... show no significant gains';
- Line 117: '... performance actually decreased slightly'.

Task 4: Identifying the writer's purpose

4.1 Answers:
The *main* function of the text is to evaluate the importance of the research.

Lines 122–123, '... pay little attention to these figures ...', indicate the evaluative/analytical content of this section. Clearly, the evaluation is critical at this stage. Lines 123–148 provide a range of reasons why research needs to be evaluated.

Lines 149–168 continue to provide a negative view of research carried out on class size. Encourage students to recognize the negative comments being used and highlight this language in the text.

The second main function of the text would appear to be a), to describe the research method.

This is shown from line 156 onwards. First the text explains the weakness of the methods being used, but then a more detailed description is given of the method used for the STAR research project (lines 168–192).

Students may also feel that the first function in the table could be considered a function of the text. Certainly, the writers express an opinion in carrying out their analysis of the research data and methods employed.

It is also important not to neglect choice b) in discussion with the class. Emphasize how research data is the vital evidence in academic work and carries far more weight than information that is purely based on impressions.

4.2 Get students to justify their choice of function(s).

Answer:
In this case, b) and d) could both be considered correct.

Explain to students that tables and figures are intended to enhance or clarify the content of the text and should not be ignored for this reason. Studying graphics and tables is another strategy to be employed when reading for quick, general understanding or decision-making about the relevance of a text.

Task 5: Understanding referencing in texts

Try to photocopy and display a section of text either on an overhead transparency (OHT) or as a handout and get students to identify referents, such as *their*, *this*, *she*, at some stage of this activity.

5.1 Answer:
a)

5.2   **Answers:**
   b)   these figures (line 123)
   c)   these data (lines 133–134)

If this is the first time that text referencing has been introduced to the students, it might be a good idea to get them to highlight the relevant words in the text and link them with arrows to the research they are referring to.

If more practice is necessary, encourage students to find further examples of referents in this section of the text and to discuss them. For example, *other factors* (line 153) refers to the information in the second paragraph; *most* (line 159) refers to 'hundreds of studies and analyses', as does *most of these studies* (line 163), *a number of studies* (line 166) and *too few* (line 167).

5.3   As it is important that students concentrate on their reading skills, encourage them to use note form and as few words as possible to indicate their answers. If the students are studying *EAS Writing*, they will be able to improve their writing when they carry out the writing assignment in the relevant unit.

   Answers:
   a)   Decreased dropout rates
   b)   Students' family commitments
   c)   Language background of students
   d)   Higher parental education level
   e)   More experienced teachers

5.4   Again, encourage students to use note form.

   Answers:
   a)   Children randomly assigned to three class sizes
   b)   The research was carried out over a number of years
   c)   Teachers randomly assigned to classes
   d)   Few teachers specially trained
   e)   No new curricular methods

Text 1-2   A case study: Shining star

Task 6: Reading a text for closer understanding (1)

6.1   **Answers:**
   There is disagreement among researchers about the benefits of class size on academic performance.
   The most succinct phrase is 'the collected findings have yielded no consensus' (lines 9–10).

6.2   **Answers:**
   a)   True   (lines 16–18)
   b)   True   (lines 20 and 32)
   c)   True   (lines 21–23)
   d)   False
   e)   True   (lines 37–40)
   f)   False   (lines 40–42)

6.3   **Answers:**
   a) 3   (but only initially) (lines 46–78)
   b) 3   (lines 49–51)
   c) 7   (lines 49–57)
   d) 7   (lines 57–67)
   e) N/A
   f) N/A

6.4   It is important to remind students regularly why they are reading this text. It is also important to discuss with students how useful this information is in terms of their real or imaginary writing assignment.

There seems to be no consensus about whether class size does impact on academic achievement. This section of the text concentrates more on ways of assessing the data than on providing information which could help answer the question.

It is very useful to discuss with students the strategies they might employ for reading this case study, especially in light of the comments (*no consensus*) made in the first paragraph.

Text 1-3 | The Asian paradox: Huge classes, high scores

Task 7: Reading a text for closer understanding (2)

7.1   Elicit from students their understanding of which are the 'developed' Asian countries. At the end of the pre-reading discussion, bring the students around to recognizing that their ideas may be *anecdotal*, unless, of course, they can provide research data.

7.3   **Answer:**
The 'Asian paradox' is *huge classes, high scores* …
The key word is *discipline* (line 19); also *discipline … from the bottom up* (lines 60–61).

7.4   **Answers:**
   • longer academic year (lines 35–37)
   • more opportunities for teachers and students to bond (lines 37–39)
   • emphasis on class, etc., as 'meaningful entities' (lines 39–42)
   • lack of 'ethnic and linguistic diversity' in Japan (lines 44–45)
   • stable family background (lines 45–47)
   • greater parental interest (lines 47–48)

7.5   Students may consider that 'bottom-up discipline', etc., is a factor that contributes to academic achievement.

Task 8: Thinking critically about the text

8.1   In particular, ask students to rate the influence of class size from the ideas they have developed. Remind students to consider factors that are directly or indirectly mentioned in the text.

Ask students to consider which reading strategy they might usefully employ for this purpose. Scanning the text might be appropriate here, as the students know what they are looking for, and which section of the text may contain the information.

8.2 Possible additions to the students' original list of influences on academic performance are:
- attracting higher-calibre teachers (page 7);
- supportive home (page 10);
- influence of teacher/teaching (page 10);
- (bottom-up) discipline; longer academic year; closer ties with teachers (page 11).

Task 9: Making use of the text

Remind students that the title of the writing assignment is:
What are the aims of academic study and how can they be achieved?

If there are Japanese students in the class, they can be used as 'experts' to verify or deny the claims made in the text. Non-Japanese students can be asked to say what they know about the situation in Japan.

Unit summary

You may wish the students to complete the unit summaries in class or in their own time. If they complete them out of class, make sure you get some feedback during class time. Whatever you choose, it might be beneficial to set up some of the activities in class, either to clarify what to do, or to help students start thinking about the topics.

Some of the items can be done individually and others are best done in pairs or groups. When working outside the classroom, encourage students to find the time to meet with others and complete any pair or group activities.

These activities encourage student reflection, so ask them to think carefully about the way they answer and share their conclusions with other students.

1   Answers:
prior, predictions, purpose, title, subheadings, selectively, understanding, critically

Web resources

UEfAP: Reading skills for academic study
A comprehensive site devoted to English for Academic Purposes. The section on reading covers microskills such as prediction, skimming and scanning (click on _efficient_) and provides practice exercises. There is also practice in identifying references (click on _understanding_).
http://www.uefap.com/reading/readfram.htm

How to read an academic article
Clarification on how academic reading is different from conventional reading. This article gives advice on how to approach a scholarly text.
http://faculty.washington.edu/davidgs/ReadArticle.html

2 Early human development

This unit will help students:

- read about human development, focusing on the relationship between nature and nurture;
- learn how to make use of the knowledge they already have about a topic before they read more;
- recognize key words and find out the meaning of difficult/unfamiliar words;
- quickly identify the main points of the text that they are reading;
- read parts of a text more carefully in order to make use of it fully according to their purposes;
- practise summarizing useful information that they have found in a text.

Text 2-1 Interaction between nature and nurture

Task 1: Assessing background knowledge

These two exercises are designed to introduce the topic and activate students' schemata in terms of prior knowledge and expectations.

Answers depend on the students.

Task 2: Vocabulary development

This task previews key vocabulary in the text. There are 20 words listed, but it is expected that students will already know some of them. Students can work on choosing the definitions in pairs or small groups. Use a class set of monolingual (English-English) dictionaries if there is one available.

Note: This task could be used as a post-reading task, depending on the level of the students. In this case, students could be encouraged to work out the meaning from context before referring to a dictionary.

2.1 Answers:

a) 8   b) 10   c) 16   d) 20   e) 7   f) 9   g) 17   h) 14   i) 6   j) 19
k) 4   l) 1   m) 3   n) 13   o) 2   p) 15   q) 5   r) 11   s) 18   t) 12

It may be useful to acquaint students with the text by getting them to search for these words, but you can skip this if you prefer.

2.2 Students may find this quite difficult, because they will need to explain the terms in their own words. Remind students that the purpose of the class is to improve their reading. Teachers should model the suggested definitions below for students to copy later if they wish.

Suggested definitions:
maturation – stages of growth not influenced by the environment
motor behaviours – movements such as sitting down, standing up, walking

Task 3: Reading for general understanding

Students read the text quickly to get an idea of the content. You may wish to set a time limit of five or six minutes for this. Students can then discuss in pairs whether, in general, their background knowledge is confirmed or contradicted by the article.

Task 4: Developing further understanding

4.1 Allow five minutes for each of these skimming tasks, which are designed to familiarize students with the main topics and ideas.

Answers:
a) Darwin – biological basis/return to hereditary viewpoint (lines 17–20)
b) Locke – see paragraph A (*tabula rasa*); the idea is also implicit in Skinner & Watson (lines 23–30)
c) Skinner & Watson – malleable/easily influenced or changed (lines 23–30)
d) Modern psychologists – paragraph C (lines 37–46)

4.2 Explain to the students that the purpose of this exercise is to familiarize them with the main topics of the second half of the text.

Answers:
a) Para F
b) Para D
c) Para H
d) Para E
e) Para G

Task 5: Understanding the main argument

Working individually, students choose a sentence, then compare and justify their answers in small groups.

Answers:
b) is correct. This is the main idea of the text.
Others are excluded because:
a) is a behaviourist view, which is not what the text is arguing;
c) is a strict nature view, which is not what the text is arguing;
d) the text does not consider modern disputes about nature vs nurture.

Task 6: Note-taking from the text

This exercise is designed to get the students to do something with the text that they might want to do for their studies. It is a first taste of reading for academic purposes. Students should concentrate on transferring relevant information from the text rather than agonizing over paraphrasing. It would be a good idea to get students to quote line numbers. Lower-level students could be directed towards the relevant paragraphs, i.e., paragraphs E–H. It has been pointed out that the answers for Task 6 provide useful information for the corresponding tasks in *EAS Writing*.

Suggested answers:

Influences of *nature* on early human development	Influences of *nurture* on early human development
Genetic structure of fertilized ovum determines sex of fetus, colour of hair, general body size, etc.	Abnormal uterine environment can affect maturation process, e.g., if mother contracts German measles.
Development (maturation) process genetically programmed.	Talking to babies encourages them to make speech-like sounds earlier.
Almost all children go through same stages of learning motor behaviours.	Infants learn to walk earlier if given stepping practice.

Task 7: Developing understanding of the text

Make sure that students understand what is meant by the term *second half* (of a century).
This task gives more gist reading practice, for those who have the time and the need for it.

Answers:
a) 1930s
b) second half of 20th century
c) 17th century; 1930s
d) 19th century
e) 20th century
f) 17th century
g) 20th century

Task 8: Working with words from the text

8.1 This is an optional exercise to consolidate the vocabulary that was pre-taught for the reading text on page 26.

There are obviously no definitive groupings for these words. The task is intended to get students to interact positively with the text and with vocabulary in general.

Possible groupings, which could be displayed for general class discussion, include:
- Parts of speech, e.g., (1) adjectives: *malleable, biological, genetic, neurological, maternal, verbal*, etc., (2) nouns, (3) verbs, etc.
- Logical (semantic) groupings, e.g., *nature, nurture, heredity, personality traits*.
- Parts of the body (or words connected with the body), e.g., *ovum, fetus*.

Text 2-2 | Capacities of the newborn

Task 9: Pre-reading discussion

Get students to discuss the question in groups, then canvass them for ideas.

Task 10: Inferring meaning from the text

It is important to give the students support in selecting key words and then constructing a brief (one sentence) summary, as this is a task they are regularly asked to do in this course. The level of support can be judged according to the needs of the students as they attempt Task 11.

a) Insist that the students do not read beyond paragraph A at this point. The writer does not state what the sensory systems are, but they are presumably the five senses: touch, taste, smell, hearing, sight. If students have difficulty coming up with something, you could mention the idea of the five senses and elicit what they are.

b) **Answer:**
They are well-prepared and ready to learn quickly.

Task 11: Summarizing information from the text (1)

11.1 Students can do this in pairs or small groups. Afterwards, they can briefly share their ideas with the rest of the class.

11.2 Students do this individually. Encourage students to focus both on the main point and examples in the text. After they have finished, establish a consensus and write it on the board.

Key words could include:
- (for the main idea): *ingenious procedures*; *change … baby's environment*; *observe … responses*
- (for the example): *tone/flashing light*; *change … heart rate*; *turns … head*; *sucks more vigorously on a nipple*; *present two stimuli*; *look longer at one than the other*

11.3 Students do this individually. Depending on the needs of the group, you may decide to write the introduction below on the board and get students to complete it. The idea contained in this is important because it explains the purpose of the psychologists' research.

Psychologists have investigated how prepared newborn babies are for learning from their new environment by …

Establish a consensus and write a model summary on the board.

Example:
Psychologists have investigated how prepared newborn babies are for learning from their new environment by designing experiments to measure the capacities of newborn babies which introduce changes in the environment, in order to observe their responses.

Task 12: Summarizing information from the text (2)

12.1 Stimulate interest by eliciting some ideas from the class.

12.2 Students do this search-reading task individually. Essentially, only paragraph D is relevant to the task, but it will be useful for students to realize this for themselves as they look at the text. You could warn them that not all of the information in paragraphs C–E is relevant. After they have finished, establish a consensus and write it on the board.

Key words could include:
(attracted to) *areas of high visual contrast*; *edges of an object*; (keep looking at) *areas that have most edges*; (prefer) *complex patterns*; (prefer) *patterns with curved lines*; (especially interested in) *faces*

12.3 Students do this individually and then compare in pairs. It may be necessary to advise students that they do not need to summarize the whole text. After they have finished, establish a consensus and write it on the board.

Example:
The features of the visual environment that most catch the attention of newborn babies are areas of high visual contrast, edges of an object, areas that have most edges, complex patterns, patterns with curved lines and especially faces.

Text 2-3 | Hearing, taste and smell

Task 13: Using background knowledge

Students do this individually. This sets them up for search-reading the text in Task 14.

Task 14: Reading for a purpose and creating a summary

14.1 After the students have search-read the text for the information they need, get them to compare what they have found out with their partners. Tell them to refer back to the text when discussing which things the writer says newborn babies can do. After this, go through the answers, dealing with problems briefly.

According to the text:
Newborn babies (aged one month or less) can do **a**, **b**, **e**, **f**, **g**, **i**, **j** and **l**. Point out that the writer does not mention the other items at all, so we don't know from looking at the text whether or not newborn babies can do them.

Problematic items: c – babies can do this at four months, not at one month or less;
f – the text refers to the human voice and other sounds, so some inferring may be required to establish that this can be done by newborn babies.

14.2 Students discuss in groups of three or four. This will involve informal verbal summarizing, which may act as a bridge to more effective written summarizing. If students are not surprised, it may simply be because they have spent a lot of time around babies, or even had babies of their own. In this case, the students concerned can be encouraged to act as an information-giving resource.

14.3 Students do this individually. Then they work with a partner from a different group to compare summaries. Students should be encouraged to focus on the main point suggested in each paragraph and to recognize the difference between main point and exemplification. For example, the main point in paragraph F is that babies have the innate ability to react to noise.

Note: The summary should be a basic, brief paraphrase of the explanation given in the text, and it may be necessary to point this out to students. The four main points are:

Answers:
- Babies react to noise.
- They can differentiate between sounds and are tuned to the properties of human speech. (These two properties may be seen as separate, in which case five rather than four innate abilities may be involved.)
- They can discriminate differences in taste.
- They can discriminate between odours.

Unit summary

1   Point out the importance of answering what is true for the students at this point in their learning. Once they have completed the questionnaire, encourage them to discuss any issues with other students on the course. It would also be useful to go over their answers as a class.

2   Note that the students might come up with different answers from those below and give reasons for their choice. However, these are the most likely.

Answers:
a) cardiac arrest   **b)** verb tenses   **c)** fracture   **d)** bus lanes   **e)** waste disposal

Web resources

Reading: Pre-reading strategies
This is a study guide aimed at teachers and high-level students. It looks at pre-reading strategies and skills such as using existing knowledge about a topic. It also explains the rationale behind pre-reading activities that students are sometimes asked to do, and suggests ways to access, organize and increase prior knowledge of a topic.
http://departments.weber.edu/teachall/reading/prereading.html

3a The environment today

This unit will help students:
- read quickly for global comprehension of the main ideas in a text;
- make use of their prior knowledge to help their global comprehension;
- identify key words to enhance quick global comprehension;
- think about what strategies to use for a specific reading purpose.

Explain to the students that they are going to work on two texts; the work they cover in the first text, *Acid rain in Norway*, will help them complete a global summary writing task relating to the second text, *Skylarks in decline*. Also explain that, as well as being relevant to their general academic reading needs, this unit will be particularly useful in helping them to read quickly and efficiently during examinations.

A problem with tasks where students are asked to summarize the text within a time limit is that they may try to read the text carefully rather than employ suitable selective reading strategies, such as skimming or search-reading. Therefore, it is suggested, in particular with the second main task (writing a global summary of *Skylarks in decline*), that a strict time limit of ten minutes be imposed. The length of time given to carry out the summary will obviously depend on the needs and level of the class.

Text 3a-1 | Acid rain in Norway

Task 1: Raising text awareness

1.1 Features of a global summary are: main ideas/theme of the whole text and a general overview of the contents of a text. It doesn't go into detail with supporting ideas and it should not include minor ideas.

1.2 Point out that the title is often, but not always, a good indicator of the main idea in a text. In this case, it introduces the topic without giving any real hint about the development of this topic. Be strict about time here. This is a schemata-raising activity. Encourage students to work together on this, particularly so that those who have never heard of acid rain can benefit from those who have.

1.3 Answers:
Typical questions might be:
- What is acid rain?
- What causes acid rain?
- Should we be concerned about acid rain?
- Where does acid rain occur?

Point out that by asking questions like these, the reader is immediately providing a purpose for reading the text, i.e., to find out the answers.

Task 2: Taking information from displayed information

2.1 Examples of the type of new information that can be obtained from this overt information are:

Information source	New information or words
Figure 1	Very sharp rise in amount of lime used to reduce acidification damage, especially since 1993
Figure 2	Sulphur dioxide emissions falling gradually 1975–1995
Figure 3	Rising nitrogen oxide emissions peaked late 1980s
Table 1	Excess sulphur deposits expected to fall over next 10 years
Section subheading A	Rivers and lakes are damaged (by acid rain)
Section subheading B	Damage can be combated/reduced

Point out that students must not simply copy the subheadings, but also describe what they deduce from these subheadings.

Explain that the amount of new information will obviously depend on the level of prior knowledge that the reader has.

2.2 Answers:

Ways of quickly accessing information about a text include:

- looking at the title;
- looking at the section headings;
- looking at figures and tables;
- looking at first and last paragraphs of texts;
- looking for topic sentences (e.g., first sentence of paragraph);
- looking at pictures and captions, etc. (there are none included with this text, but it is worth mentioning).

It is important to round this off with the whole class so that they can discuss and reach a general agreement. Display ideas on the whiteboard or an OHT so that everyone can note ideas that they had not thought of.

Task 3: Writing a global summary

Before students begin this task, point out that during the process of summarizing it is often more effective to summarize in your own words.

3.1 It may be necessary to remind students that they will not have time to read the whole text and that they should make use of some or all of the strategies that have been brainstormed above.

3.2 Be reasonably strict about the time limit. When the time is up, ask how many students have completed the summary, and ask those who have not finished why they think this might be. This may lead to a general discussion about whether the students, in fact, followed the procedures discussed in Ex 3.1 above.

If students have found this task difficult, you might carry out some remedial work in the following way. First elicit and display some appropriate terms on the board, e.g., *acid rain, sulphur dioxide, lime, acidification, fish, international agreements, emission levels, long term, permanent, short term*. With weaker groups, list some terms and elicit other terms to add to the list. You could write up SITUATION-PROBLEMS-SOLUTIONS and get students to match the terms to these categories. From this point, you could either get students to attempt the summary again, making use of the key points that have been introduced, or you could demonstrate writing a summary yourself using the key points. This could then be compared to the suggested answer (see below).

3.3 Display the following model summary for comparison. Explain that when writing a summary, incorrect spelling, punctuation and even grammar are not important, as long as the summary can be understood without undue difficulty. It is also important to stress that the following is just a model and is not necessarily the only suitable summary. Encourage students to compare the model with their own summary and make suggestions for changing the content of the model summary, if appropriate. (This model is repeated on page 39 of this book to facilitate copying.)

Model summary of *Acid rain in Norway*
Acid rain, often coming from other countries, has caused serious problems in Norway, such as the widespread destruction of fish. The problem is being dealt with through the application of lime to affected areas and through the introduction of international agreements to reduce emission levels of toxic acids. However, no permanent solution will be achieved until the emission levels of both nitrogen oxides and sulphur dioxide are reduced. The critical loads approach to dealing with acid rain emissions has already had some impact on the problem faced by Norway, specifically with the reduction of sulphur deposits (Middleton, 1998).

Middleton, N. (1998). Acid rain in Norway. *Geography Review*, 11(4), 16–17.

3.4–3.6 Ex 3.4–3.5 are intended to encourage students to reflect on the way they have carried out the summarizing task above and how successful they have been. It may be appropriate to repeat these tasks after students have written a summary of *Skylarks in decline*.

Text 3a-2 | Skylarks in decline

Task 4: More global summary practice

4.1/4.2 Be strict with the timing of this task. Collect the summaries after the students have finished, to ensure that they strictly observe the time limit. You could then check through their summaries to see whether they have included all or some of the key points, or you may decide to go straight to comparing their summaries with the model (see below).

4.3 Display the following model answer for comparison. It is again important to stress that the following is just a model and is not necessarily the only suitable summary. Encourage students to compare the model with their own summaries and make suggestions for changing the content of the model summary if appropriate. (This model is repeated on page 40 of this book to facilitate copying.)

Model summary of *Skylarks in decline*
The skylark population has decreased dramatically over a 20-year period in lowland farming areas of Britain. It is thought that changes in agricultural practices have had a significant impact on the nesting, feeding and breeding habits of the skylark. This may also account for the decline of other common farmland species. Monocultural practices, the use of pesticides and changes in planting routines, etc., have all disturbed the natural habitat of the skylark. The problem may be reduced by adjusting farming routines, such as setting aside land not to be used for production. Research into which conditions of farming and types of farming cause decline and which may improve skylark numbers is being carried out (Everett, 1997).

Everett, M. (1997). Skylarks in decline. *Biological Sciences*, 10(2), 7–9.

4.4   Possible answers:

a) Some of the ways in which *Skylarks in decline* is **similar** to *Acid rain in Norway* include:
- The topic is clear from the title, section headings, figures.
- Both come from journals/magazines.

Some of the ways in which *Skylarks in decline* is **different** from *Acid rain in Norway* include:
- The figure in *Skylarks in decline* includes more written information underneath.
- There is no table with *Skylarks in decline*.
- In some paragraphs of *Skylarks in decline*, the main idea/topic sentence does not appear at the beginning of the paragraph, e.g., line 120. Line 124 is clearly not the topic sentence of the paragraph, it simply sets the scene, and the second sentence adds to this scene-setting. The third sentence, beginning line 130, seems to contain the main idea.

b) and c) Encourage the students to reflect on their work and discuss any issues raised as a class.

Unit summary

1   Answers:
topic, word, title or heading, prior, questions, information, key

Encourage the students to discuss activities 2 and 3 with their fellow students.

Web resources

The owl at Purdue: Quoting, paraphrasing, and summarizing
A site that gives tips and pointers and provides practice in paraphrasing and summarizing.
http://owl.english.purdue.edu/owl/resource/563/01/

Model summary of *Acid rain in Norway*

Acid rain, often coming from other countries, has caused serious problems in Norway, such as the widespread destruction of fish. The problem is being dealt with through the application of lime to affected areas and through the introduction of international agreements to reduce emission levels of toxic acids. However, no permanent solution will be achieved until the emission levels of both nitrogen oxides and sulphur dioxide are reduced. The critical loads approach to dealing with acid rain emissions has already had some impact on the problem faced by Norway, specifically with the reduction of sulphur deposits (Middleton, 1998).

Middleton, N. (1998). Acid rain in Norway. *Geography Review*, 11(4), 16–17.

Model summary of *Skylarks in decline*

The skylark population has decreased dramatically over a 20-year period in lowland farming areas of Britain. It is thought that changes in agricultural practices have had a significant impact on the nesting, feeding and breeding habits of the skylark. This may also account for the decline of other common farmland species. Monocultural practices, the use of pesticides and changes in planting routines, etc., have all disturbed the natural habitat of the skylark. The problem may be reduced by adjusting farming routines, such as setting aside land not to be used for production. Research into which conditions of farming and types of farming cause decline and which may improve skylark numbers is being carried out (Everett, 1997).

Everett, M. (1997). Skylarks in decline. *Biological Sciences*, 10(2), 7–9.

4 Statistics without tears

This unit will help students:
- practise reading to acquire knowledge;
- learn how to distinguish between main and minor points in a text;
- summarize information from short sections of a text.

This unit is designed to improve the following three aspects of students' reading:

- *Reading to acquire knowledge*. One of the main strands of this course is to encourage and provide guidance and practice in *reading to learn*, i.e., acquiring information from a text for a given academic purpose. This unit takes a general approach to this, in the sense that the main purpose for reading in this case is to get a preliminary understanding of a new topic from an introductory text. An example of when students might do this is initial background reading prior to attending a course of lectures on a particular topic. In such circumstances, reading often follows the order of exposition of the writer and does not involve selective reading.

- *Distinguishing between main and minor points in a text*. This is an important general reading skill, applicable to a range of reading purposes.

- *Summarizing information from short sections of a text*. An example of when students might do this is when they take initial notes in preparation for an exam to be taken later on in the course. At this stage, we are not too concerned with paraphrasing skills; the emphasis is more on understanding the main points, regardless of the form of words used.

Text 4-1 Making sense of experience

Task 1: Statistics in practice

These tasks are designed to prepare students for reading about the topic of statistics. The idea of the discussion questions is to encourage students to start thinking statistically in an informal way before they look at a more formal account. This helps to personalize their experience of reading the text.

The tasks should be completed fairly quickly, and you may wish to explain vocabulary to weaker groups to keep things moving. For example, you may need to explain and/or demonstrate the meaning of *heads* and *tails*. Students may produce some of the language associated with making deductions during their discussions, e.g., *probably*, *possibly*, *maybe* and a number of appropriate modals, and you may wish to emphasize such language as you monitor their speaking.

After the group discussions, get groups to feed back to the whole class. At this stage, explore ways in which answers suggested by students might not be correct. Possible responses for each situation follow:

a) We might expect that Kate arrived at 9 o'clock on Friday because this follows the pattern established from Monday to Thursday. However, there could be several reasons why Kate did not arrive at the predicted time on Friday. For example, it might have taken her longer to get to work because of a hold-up in the traffic, or because she always starts earlier or later on a Friday.

b) We might expect to see heads on both sides of the coin. Students might answer that it is a 'double-headed' coin. (You may wish to explain this term.)

It is, of course, possible in principle for heads to come up six times in succession with a normal coin. However, the fact that the person tossing the coin is performing a magic trick and is confident of the outcome, suggests that the conclusion that a double-headed coin is being used is more likely to be correct.

Task 2: Identifying main and supporting points

You will notice that the text in the Source Book has been arranged so that each section of the text begins on a new page. Students should not continue reading until they have answered the question asked by the author. Reading on after answering these questions, the students will be able to compare their answers with the next section of the text, which provides the author's answer. Thus, the students are encouraged to interact with the text.

The introduction to Task 2 states that the discussion questions involve 'everyday statistical thinking'. You may wish to clarify this by saying that the predictions involved are made on the basis of common patterns that people observe, e.g., somebody arriving at work at the same time for four days in a row; typical variations between heads and tails when tossing a coin repeatedly.

2.1/2.2 **Answers:**
Students may feel that c) is a main point, but it is an example of b).
f) is an example of d).
All are main points except c) and f).

2.3 Students write their answers. Stress that they need to understand the text well up to that point before they try to answer the question, and that they should keep their answers as brief as possible.

After the students have read the first section of this text, ask them whether they think it is typically 'academic' in terms of the language used and the style – clearly, this isn't the case. Ask students to identify features of the text which are not typically academic.

Non-academic features include:
- the length of the paragraphs (very short, single-sentence paragraphs towards the end of the section);
- the 'closeness' of the writer to the reader (typically, academic writing tends to display 'distance' between writer and reader – this can be achieved through passivization and use of the third person).

Ask the students why the writer may have chosen to use the style he has with a relatively serious topic. The probable answer is that he wants to make the text accessible to a wider reading community.

Encourage students to look for other examples of non-academic features in this text as they read later sections, such as contractions *shouldn't/we'll*, etc. It is worth mentioning, however, that although the language/vocabulary used is not particularly formal, it is neutral rather than informal.

Task 3: Continuing to identify main and minor points

3.1 It is important to discourage students from looking ahead to this section *before* they have completed Task 2. Explain the importance of interacting with the text and personalizing their understanding and reaction to the views and contents expressed. It is also crucial for the students to understand that the writer is expressing a *possible* response (line 31: We <u>might</u> ask …).

3.2 Answers:
a), b) and c) are main points;
d) and e) are examples of generalizations.

3.3 Students write their answers. Stress that they need to understand the text well up to that point before they try to answer the question, and that they should keep their answers as brief as possible.

Task 4: Summarizing the key points (1)

4.1 Tell students that if they are not sure about the writer's answer, they should ask you to help them. While individual students do this, allow other students to continue reading this section. The technique of having a class reading a text while you help individual students with their problems is suggested for the first time in this task, but it is a good idea to use this technique whenever students are working on long texts.

The following comments may help you give appropriate support to those who need it:
- The writer is urging the reader to be cautious about making generalizations because of the many possible variables that might have affected the field with the bigger crop, such as the weather, and the variables that might influence crop size in other fields.
- If a student has mentioned other variables in their answers, reassure them that this is not a problem, because the writer has decided to mention only certain examples.
- If a student thinks it would be safe to generalize in this way, it may be necessary to refer her/him back to the previous section.

4.2/4.3 The aim of this task is to provide scaffolding to help students produce more independent summaries of the main points of the text. The words and phrases in the box provide five correct answers and five distractors (which are syntactically possible, but are not what the writer says). If students experience difficulties in identifying the correct answers, refer them back to the text and encourage them to find the appropriate sections in the text relating to each point and then discuss the answers in relation to these.

Some students may be able to complete this task without further reference to the text. However, it would be useful for them to go back to the text to check their answers before the class plenary.

Answers:
a) 2   **b)** 7   **c)** 6   **d)** 8   **e)** 1

4.4 Students write their answers. Stress that they need to understand the text well up to that point before they try to answer the question, and that they should keep their answers as brief as possible.

Task 5: Summarizing the key points (2)

5.1 See comments for Task 4 above.

5.2 This task provides less scaffolding than Task 4 and practises summarizing for gist. It is important to point out to students that the words they need to complete the skeleton summary are in the text. If students experience difficulties in identifying the correct answers, refer them back to the text and encourage them to find the appropriate sections relating to each point, and then discuss the answers in relation to these.

Some students may be able to complete this task without further reference to the text. However, it would be useful for them to go back to the text to check their answers before the class plenary.

Answers:
reliable, individuals, experience, estimates/predictions

Text 4-2 | What is statistics?

Task 6: Concentrating on the main points

This task practises selecting the main points, with more limited scaffolding. This is intended to provide an introduction to the less-controlled reading tasks that will appear later in the course.

In lines 90–104, the main points appear in the first nine lines of text and the main ideas that students should note are basically the italicized phrases. The following lines, 105–109, explain these main points.

The key ideas are:
* a whole subject or discipline;
* methods used to collect, process or interpret quantitative data;
* collections of data (gathered by those methods);
* specially calculated figures (that characterize such a collection of data).

In lines 110–122, it could be argued that the only main point, apart from the one given to the students as an example, is:
* Most academic disciplines use statistics to a greater or lesser degree.

The remainder of this paragraph gives examples of how statistics is put to use as a *ubiquitous tool of systematic research*.

In lines 123–140, the main points that students should note are:
* Statistical thinking is a way of recognizing that our observations of the world can never be totally accurate …
* Statistics enables us to measure the extent of our errors.

For lower-level classes, you may prefer to use the alternative version of this exercise, which appears on page 48 of this book. You will need to photocopy the task for your students as it is not in the Course Book.

The alternative task (see page 48):
There is certainly room for discussion with students concerning which of the points listed are main points, which are minor points and which are examples.
A possible route for lower-level students is to proceed as follows:
* Read the next section of *What is statistics?* and decide what the main idea(s) are in each paragraph. Make a list of these.
* Compare your list with other students.
* In pairs, compare your lists with the answers supplied by your teacher.

Answers:
The **main points** are a)–e), g), h), j) and l). It could be argued that b)–e) are **sub-main points** of a); however, they are so important to the general understanding of the text that they should be considered **main points** in their own right. g) and h) might be considered as a **single main**

point, but h) introduces the importance of statistics in a specifically academic context and therefore should be considered a **main point** on its own.

The **minor points or examples** are f), which exemplifies how a researcher might use statistics as a resource, and expands on e); i), which is an example of a particular technique or tool employed by certain academics/scientists; k), which expands further on main point j); and m), which expands on main point l).

Text 4-3 | Descriptive and inferential statistics

Task 7: Note-taking practice

7.1/7.2 Students write their answers. Stress that they need to understand the text well up to that point before they try to answer the question, and that they should keep their answers as brief as possible.

7.3 The **answer** is clearly stated at the beginning of Section 7:

Statement (i) is descriptive (an attempt to summarize experience), while (ii) and (iii) go beyond what is likely to happen in the future.

There are two very short one-sentence paragraphs at this point, and it is worth drawing the students' attention to the second of these (lines 156–158), which is important for their general understanding of the text.

7.4/7.5 This section of the unit provides far less scaffolding and gives the opportunity for students to work more independently. Draw their attention to the instruction here so that they have a clear purpose for reading the text, i.e., to draw a distinction between *descriptive and inferential statistics and to find out what the writer has to say about the reliability of making generalizations.*

The students are asked to write a summary based on this for Ex 8.3 in Task 8. Students may decide to read straight through the text and then make notes, or they may prefer to underline or annotate the text as they are reading and then reread to confirm their choice of relevant material. Reading is an individualistic activity, so allow students to follow the style of reading they prefer.

You may like to have a brief discussion at the end of this activity about how the students carried out their reading. As you monitor their reading, it is important to assess from their note-taking whether they are keeping their purpose for reading in mind.

Task 8: Recalling information from the text

8.1/8.2 This recall activity is intended to help students personalize the text, and it does provide some scaffolding. Pair off students as they finish Task 7 and explain to them that recalling a text will help them to understand it more fully and in a more personal way. They should only refer to the text to confirm their understanding, or to resolve any disagreements that may crop up during their recalling of the relevant points. Remind students to stick to their original purpose for reading the text as they work on this activity.

8.3 Initially, students should work independently on this task. Explain that information has to be *relevant*, *concise* and *understandable* without immediate further explanation. Monitor students to ensure that they are keeping to the point. Prevent students from agonizing over language by stressing that this is a reading activity. Don't insist on the students writing in note-form, because earlier in this unit they have been basically lifting sentences/phrases from the text.

8.4 During this comparison stage, students should refer to the text as necessary and concentrate on text content and relevance.

8.5 On page 49 of this book there is a model summary of this section of the text. It would be a good idea to make an OHT of this summary and provide students with handouts. Draw the students' attention to the two questions displayed above the model summary:
- *How does it compare to yours?*
- *Do you think it contains the most important points, or are there important things missing?*

Encourage students to be critical of the model summary if they wish. There are examples listed in the model and students might discuss how appropriate this is, given that their main purpose is to summarize main points. You could point out that the examples, *white mice*, etc., are simply included for reference, and not expanded on.

Task 9: How to summarize a text appropriately

Note: This supplementary task is printed on page 50 of this book for ease of photocopying.

This may be used as a *supplementary* task, depending on students' level and needs. You may feel, however, that it offers a useful opportunity for all students to consolidate their skills in deciding how to approach a particular piece of reading. Your decision about this will depend very much on the level and needs of the students you are teaching. It would be a good idea to draw up a list of points that they consider either very important or quite important, in collaboration with the students.

Possible answers:
Three factors are **very** important:
1 Background knowledge of the reader;
2 Purpose of summary;
3 Time available for reading/summary.

The following are **quite** important:
4 Text difficulty – of language and content (ideas);
5 Text type – purpose and organization; topic; amount of detail contained;
6 Summarizing ability of the reader.

Finally, encourage a general discussion about these factors, and how they might influence the level of detail (or even, in some cases, the basic nature) of a summary.

Unit summary

1   Answer:
main, key, important; minor, supporting

2   Answers:
Growing populations in the world's biggest cities: b)
Sports injuries: a)

Web resources

Rio Hondo: Reading tips
Students can go to the sections on *locating the main idea* and *major and minor details* for more practice in identifying the main idea in a text. It also has a section on how to read graphs. http://faculty.riohondo.edu/dkaller/readingtips/majordet.htm

Econoclass: statistics can be misleading
This site encourages students to look at a range of authentic US statistics in graphs, charts and news articles, and work out why they are misleading. http://www.econoclass.com/misleadingstats.html

Alternative Task 6

You are going to read a section of *What is statistics?*

Read this section and decide which of the following are **main points (main)** and which are **minor points or examples (minor)**.

When you have finished, compare your list with those of the other members of your group.

a) The word *statistics* is used in four different senses.

b) Firstly, it refers to a subject of study.

c) Secondly, it refers to methods used to collect and interpret data.

d) Thirdly, it refers to collections of data.

e) Fourthly, it refers to special figures that have been calculated from collections of data.

f) A researcher in the statistics department of a firm may quote statistics about sales of a new detergent.

g) Most professional activities use statistical thinking.

h) Statistics is used by most academic disciplines, including sciences, humanities and literary studies.

i) Radio-carbon dating is a statistical technique.

j) Statistics is used because of our uncertainty about what we observe in the world around us.

k) We can use statistics to predict the average height of school children in one class by using our knowledge of the average height of children in another class.

l) Statistics allows us to estimate the extent of our errors.

m) We may be almost certain about what a certain child's height is to the nearest half inch.

Descriptive and inferential statistics and the reliability of making generalizations

Consider the following summary. How does it compare to yours? Do you think it contains the most important points, or are there important things missing?

1 Important distinction between:
- descriptive statistics – summarizes experience/observations
- inferential statistics – predictions for the future based on descriptive stats

2 Another important distinction between:
- population – complete group that researcher wants generalizations/ predictions to apply to (e.g., all white mice, all people, all light bulbs)
- sample – smaller group taken from population to collect observations and do statistics

Idea is that stats done on sample will lead to useful generalizations regarding the population researcher is interested in.

3 Very important to make sample as representative of population as possible (= as similar to population as possible, apart from smaller group size). Reliability of generalizations depends on how representative sample is. Incorrect generalizations often caused by lack of representativeness (even with professional researchers).

How to summarize a text appropriately

Writing a summary

Consider the following:

1   What is the appropriate level of detail for a summary?

2   Is it always the same or does it depend on certain factors?

3   If the latter, what are the factors, and how do they determine the level of detail required?

4   Be specific – e.g., in situation **a**, *x level* is appropriate, whereas in **b**, *y level* is appropriate.

Brainstorm some ideas, discuss them with your teacher, and compile a class list of useful points. Keep a record of this.

5 Human activity and climate change

This unit will help students:
- learn how to overview a text before reading, to assess its value;
- read selectively to identify words that might provide relevant information;
- practise *writing into reading* as a technique for increasing understanding of a text;
- identify topic sentences in a paragraph and recognize the supporting sentences;
- learn text-mapping as a means of enhancing understanding;
- make use of graphs, figures and tables to increase understanding of content.

This unit focuses on *reading to acquire knowledge* and develops the 'reading to learn' strand of the course. There is emphasis on the fact that students will already have a knowledge base to call on to help with their reading comprehension. They are encouraged to use the text to *confirm their existing knowledge and to develop it further*. This is particularly relevant with this unit topic because many students may already know quite a lot about the effects of global warming.

Students are encouraged to make decisions about which of the three sections of the unit are specifically relevant to the Focus task, preparing to write an essay or to give an oral presentation on the topic: *What role has human activity played in causing climate change?*, as well as about which parts of the sections are relevant.

Text 5-1 | Extra-textual information

Task 1: Overviewing the text

1.1 Answers:
Other ways of overviewing a text include:
- studying the title and headings;
- referring to diagrams, tables and other graphics;
- checking the contents page;
- checking through the conclusion;
- reading the abstract, i.e., *a short piece of writing providing the main points of an article or other document.*

Overviewing the text:
Point out to students that it is important to look carefully at figures and diagrams to assess their relevance to a task. Encourage students to think about the figure in each section of the texts in this unit and to decide whether each seems to be relevant to the Focus task.
- Again, the diagrams vary in complexity and relevance to the students' needs. Figure 1.1, for example, is relatively straightforward and could be a source of useful vocabulary. There is some relevant information displayed in this diagram.
- Figure 2.1 is much more complex, and the non-expert reader would have to read the accompanying text carefully to learn from the diagram. Students might decide that this figure is too complex or inaccessible to worry too much about. Reassure them that this is often the case with first-language English-speaking readers as well.
- Figure 3.1 is not obviously useful, but can be very useful if read in conjunction with the text. Point out to students that figures and diagrams only serve a useful purpose if they add to the contents of the text in some way, e.g., by summarizing the contents or clarifying them to the reader.
- Figure 3.2 is not obviously useful to the reader in terms of the Focus task, but explain that its usefulness may well depend on how the reader decides to use the information in the diagram.

1.2 You are advised to spend no more than ten minutes on this activity.

Answers:

a) Students may opt for the title *Common questions about climate change*, or may suggest a more technical description, e.g., *Meteorology, Global warming* or simply *Climate change*.

b) By referring to the details printed on the first page, students should recognize that a range of authors has been involved in contributing to the brochure. They should notice that a raft of expertise has been recruited to add weight to the information contained in the document. Students may point out that the authors involved are virtually all from the USA or the UK, which they may feel detracts from the credibility of the information, i.e., that it is Western. This is a reasonable observation, but it is worth pointing out the role of reviewers and contributors who come from a wide range of countries. Also explain that the sections of text students are going to read form only part of a much larger document and this helps to explain why there are so many authors listed.

c) The text could have been written to inform/describe/explain. There is certainly an overlap between these reasons. It is also reasonable to suggest that the writers want to state an opinion and therefore persuade their readers.

d) The text is academic in that the sentences are generally quite long and complex, and the language is fairly technical. The passive voice is used regularly. Get students to spot examples of the above.

e) Having done an overview of the whole text is clearly essential for answering this question. However, you may need to remind students what the actual essay title is:
What role has human activity played in causing climate change?

Task 2: Writing into reading

2.1/2.2 Give examples of, or demonstrate, listing (e.g., shopping list, telephone directory, team sheet). The emphasis should be on completing the reading task, so any writing should occupy as little time as possible. Students may tend to provide specific examples, e.g., *slash and burn farming methods as practised in Africa, factory fumes*. Therefore, encourage them to generalize such examples, e.g., *land use, burning fossil fuel*.

The reason for getting students to tick examples of personal experience is to encourage them to personalize the text, which is regarded as an effective means of improving reading skills.

2.3 Figure 1.1 provides some relevant information. Also refer to lines 37–54.

Encourage students to add to their lists in note-form if appropriate – this will help with completion of the Focus task.

Text 5-2 | Common questions about climate change

Task 3: Identifying topic sentences

This task is intended for general discussion.

a) **Answer:**
Topic sentences tend to appear at the beginning of a paragraph, but when a paragraph develops the contents of earlier text, the 'topic' is often implied rather than directly stated.

b) **Answer:**
They explain, develop or clarify the topic, e.g., by providing examples. The second paragraph provides an example of this. This is developed further in Task 5.

Task 4: Understanding the general meaning of a text

4.1 **Answers:**
Definition of climate (1); Climate versus weather (2); Processes influencing climate (3)

4.2 **Answers:**
- Paragraph B = (1) and (2)
- Paragraph C = (3) '(long-term) balance of energy of the Earth and its atmosphere'
- Paragraph D = (3) role of winds and oceans
- Paragraph E = (3) role of natural events, for example, volcanic eruptions and variations in ocean currents, e.g., El Niño (short-term) and 'natural changes in the geographical distribution of energy' (long-term), i.e., solar, greenhouse gases and atmospheric dust
- Paragraphs F–I = (3) role of human activities, i.e., increased amount of greenhouse gases < land use, burning fossil fuels, etc.

4.3 **Answer:**
Paragraph G ('… human activities will change the climate by …'); paragraph H (details of temperature increases and likely effects).

4.4 **Answer:**
It explains the intergovernmental response to climate change, the significance of the IPPC reports (1990 and 1996) and outlines the purpose of the document *Common questions about climate change*.

Task 5: Topic sentences and supporting sentences

5.1 The organization of the paragraphs in this section tend to follow a common pattern. The topic sentence occupies the initial position in most instances. Paragraph A is explained to the students. Paragraphs G and H expand on the role of 'human activity' through explanation and detail. Paragraph E concentrates on a comparison between the relatively short- and long-term consequences of 'natural events'.

5.2 Depending on time and the needs of the group, spend some time looking at a few paragraphs and getting students to identify the topic sentences and the function of the accompanying sentences.

Answers:
a) It carries the main idea of the paragraph.
b) It introduces the document.

5.3 If students have problems with this task, and depending on level, first get them to identify where in the text the information occurs, and then work out whether they are main or supporting ideas. Point out that sentences a)–h) in the Course Book correspond with paragraphs B–I in the Source Book.

Answers:

a) = B	**e)** = A
b) = B	**f)** = A
c) = A	**g)** = B
d) = B	**h)** = B

These are worth discussion, and students are entitled to their own views about the role of particular ideas or details in the text.

Task 6: Recalling the text

6.1/6.3 These text-recalling tasks can be done in one of two ways: the students either make a written list of the points they have remembered and then compare it with a partner or, if time is short, they work in pairs; one student orally recalls what s/he can remember, the other student interjects at appropriate points with added information.

It is important that students see the logic of these tasks. Explain to them that recalling a text enhances understanding and is a strategy for self-monitoring of understanding.

6.4 The answer to this is arguably subjective, i.e., there is an argument that by referring to other causes of climate change, readers can, for example, minimize the impact of human activities.

Text 5-3 | Are human activities contributing to climate change?

Task 7: Identifying relevant information in a text

7.1 Ask students to use a reading strategy that will help them to decide quickly whether the contents of this section are relevant to their needs.

7.2 **Answer:**
… there has been a discernible human influence on global climate. (lines 2–3)

7.3 **Answer:**
scientific evidence (line 1)

7.4 **Answer:**
Paragraphs B, G, J, K and L are all directly or indirectly useful (see Ex 7.5 and 7.6 below).

7.5 **Answer:**
Paragraph B (lines 4–10); paragraph G ('The human factors include …', lines 36–37); paragraph J (lines 51–53)

7.6 **Answer:**
Paragraphs K and L (implications – lines 59–72)

7.7 **Answer:**
See lines 4–10. Natural changes, e.g., interactions between winds and oceans (internal factors), and external causes, such as variations in the sun's energy output and the amount of particles in the atmosphere resulting from volcanic eruptions.

This section of the text explains that scientists have to differentiate between natural and man-made causes of climate change in assessing the impact of human activity.

7.8 **Answer:**
'Early work' – line 21; 'roughly' – line 23

7.9 **Answer:**
An increasing agreement between data based on model predictions and 'observed' patterns of climate change (lines 61–62).

Task 8: Detailed reading

8.1 Answer:

It outlines the methods used for determining the contribution of human activities, i.e., under the general heading of *attribution*.

Point out to students that a description of the methods used in carrying out research is frequently included in academic papers. Explain the difference between *detection studies* and *attribution studies*, i.e., detection studies involve identifying a problem, whereas attribution studies involve either suggesting or proving what the causes of the problem are. The text differentiates between detection and attribution using a medical analogy (see paragraph D). Get students to explain this in their own words.

8.2 Answers:

Studying climate change

Studying the causes of unusual climate change is problematic because change caused by human activity is often hidden or masked by natural climate variability. In order to separate these two factors, investigations can be divided into detection and attribution studies. In the first case, information can be gained by measuring climate change, and in the second situation by finding reasons for the unusual changes in climate that have been noted. In attributing causes resulting from human activity, scientists can make use of climate models. Two examples of this are, firstly, by comparing maps or patterns of temperature change, which is known as pattern analysis, or secondly, by finding characteristic patterns of climate response between observed climate change and predicted change from models, which is referred to as a fingerprint match.

Note: This answer key is repeated on page 58 for photocopying purposes.

Task 9: Recalling the text from memory

The key points below can be displayed for comparison on an OHP or a handout.

Note: This answer key is repeated on page 59 for photocopying purposes.

Possible answer:

Climate changes caused by human activity
- Burning fossil fuels, deforestation, etc.

Natural changes:
- Internal factors (interaction between atmosphere and oceans, etc.)
- External factors (changes in the sun's energy output, etc.)

Studies:
- Detection, attribution, globally averaged surface temperature of Earth, observations in upper atmosphere (radiosondes and satellites), but need to obtain 'definitive' information (not 'satisfactory'), climate models, etc.
- Signal – human-induced > increased atmospheric concentrations of greenhouse gases and aerosol particles. Imperfect knowledge of true climate change signal (human), background noise of natural climatic variability.
- Space and time studies, e.g., pattern analysis and fingerprint matching.
- Discernible influence of human activities detected at present/likely to have future influence.
- Background noise – solar variability, volcanic eruptions (external and internal factors).

Task 10: Making use of figures and tables

10.1 Students should be encouraged to summarize the contents of Figure 3.1 orally. The language of comparison might require some revision/consolidation, depending on the level of the group, e.g., *Carbon dioxide has a much greater warming effect than methane; almost three times as great.* Refer to Swan, M., & Walter, C. (2009) *The good grammar book*. Oxford: OUP (esp pp. 208–213).

10.2 Students can infer that the greenhouse gases, which are displayed, have resulted from human activity. This has been covered in an earlier section, but may need to be revised.

10.3 Encourage students to scan the text for mention of the various greenhouse gases and for confirmation that the information in Figure 3.1 does indeed clarify or summarize the contents of the text.

Task 11: Reading displayed information

a) **Answer:**
There has been an increasingly significant rise in all three groups of countries. The increase was much greater in the latter part of the 20th century.

b) **Answer:**
The rest of the world.
It would be worth defining the groups and getting students to suggest reasons for the differences. This kind of activity encourages students to personalize their understanding of the text.

c) **Answer:**
A decrease in emissions from the more developed areas. The increases previously recorded in these areas have levelled off since around the mid-1970s.

Task 12: Inferring meaning from a text

12.1 **Answers:**
a) reduction of carbon dioxide in the atmosphere
b) significant increase in carbon dioxide (NB: compare with use of fossil fuels)
c) banning of CFCs, but substitutes likely to cause future global warming
d) significant contributor – long-term effects uncertain
e) cooling effect
f) possible cooling effect – further research necessary

Task 13: Making use of a text

If this reading course is being used in conjunction with *EAS Writing*, then the focus question *What role has human activity played in causing climate change?* can be used to carry out the assignment in the writing materials.

Alternatively, students can be encouraged to give an oral presentation.

The key thing is that students should produce a set of notes which could be used for either activity.

Unit summary

2   Answers:
   a) 5   **b)** 4   **c)** 3   **d)** 2   **e)** 7   **f)** 8   **g)** 1   **h)** 6

Web resources

California Polytechnic State University: Study skills: note-taking systems
This site gives an overview of five different note-taking systems and looks at the advantages and disadvantages of each one. http://www.sas.calpoly.edu/asc/ssl/notetaking.systems.html

BBC Learning English: Talk about English: climate change
The BBC world service programmes for learners of English have several which discuss the issues and language connected with climate change. This webcast is an audio discussion that examines key issues. http://www.bbc.co.uk/worldservice/learningenglish/webcast/070426_climate_change/

Monash University: Reading
A comprehensive site that includes tasks to help students with tasks such as note-taking and reading problems and strategies. http://www.monash.edu.au/lls/llonline/reading/index.xml

Studying climate change

Studying the causes of unusual climate change is problematic because change caused by <u>human activity</u> is often hidden or masked by natural climate variability. In order to separate these two factors, investigations can be divided into <u>detection</u> and <u>attribution</u> studies. In the first case, information can be gained by measuring <u>climate change</u>, and in the second situation by finding reasons for the unusual changes in climate that have been noted. In attributing causes resulting from human activity, scientists can make use of <u>climate models</u>. Two examples of this are, firstly, by comparing maps or patterns of temperature change, which is known as <u>pattern analysis</u>, or secondly, by finding characteristic patterns of climate response between observed climate change and predicted change from models, which is referred to as a <u>fingerprint match</u>.

Photocopiable

Climate change caused by human activity

- Burning fossil fuels, deforestation, etc.

Natural changes:
- Internal factors (interaction between atmosphere and oceans, etc.)
- External factors (changes in the sun's energy output, etc.)

Studies:
- Detection, attribution, globally averaged surface temperature of Earth, observations in upper atmosphere (radiosondes and satellites), but need to obtain 'definitive' information (not 'satisfactory'), climate models, etc.
- Signal – human-induced > increased atmospheric concentrations of greenhouse gases and aerosol particles. Imperfect knowledge of true climate change signal (human), background noise of natural climatic variability.
- Space and time studies, e.g., pattern analysis and fingerprint matching.
- Discernible influence of human activities detected at present/likely to have future influence.
- Background noise – solar variability, volcanic eruptions (external and internal factors).

6 The global village

This unit will help students:
- practise recognizing main points in a text;
- read for a specific purpose;
- analyze the titles, subtitles (subheadings) and other displayed accompanying information;
- recall the text to consolidate their understanding;
- compare their views (as a reader) with those of the writer;
- monitor their understanding of the text while they are reading.

The main focus of this unit is the preparation by the students of a two-paragraph answer to the question **Has social diversity generally increased as the result of economic globalization?** The task is designed to get students to focus on certain information in the text, allowing them to exploit a large amount of textual material in an efficient and manageable way. The first two texts, *Introduction* and *The shrinking planet*, and the accompanying tasks on pages 56–61 in the Course Book, provide support for students gathering information to answer the question. Further supporting activities are provided with Texts 3 and 4, *Economic globalization* and *Community & conflict* (pages 61–65 of the Course Book).

The last two texts, however, *The sharing of sovereignty* and *Converging or diverging?* are intended purely for students to refer to as needed. Scaffolding is deliberately withdrawn at this stage to provide a reading situation that is more authentic as far as academic reading on degree courses is concerned. The students are offered the choice of whether to use these texts or not to answer the question. The unit also accommodates students within the same group progressing at different speeds (see the section headed *Notes on Texts 6-4, 6-5, and 6-6* on page 66 of this book).

Text 6-1 | Introduction

Task 1: Pre-reading discussion

1.1 It may be necessary to encourage students with no knowledge of the term *global village* to look at the two words separately, i.e., *global* and *village* and discuss the meaning of the term from that angle. You may think it appropriate to introduce related terms, such as *globalization* and *globalized* at this point.

Either display or dictate the following definition, which comes from the same source as the texts used in this unit:
The global village means different things to different people – universal neighbourliness, mass tourism, global television and the Internet, the wide dispersion of foreign-made goods, the 'outsourcing' of business production, the power of the money markets and multinational companies, global concerns over human rights and the environment ...
(*Understanding Global Issues* 98/7)

1.2/1.3 Spend a limited amount of time on this, but try to ensure that each student has enough points on their list to carry out Task 2. Students may simply make reference to the definition printed above and/or have their own ideas, e.g., studying abroad.

Task 2: Checking predictions

Make sure that students understand the term *globalization*. It is actually quite difficult to define. The following definitions may help:
- a process by which activities go beyond national boundaries (*internationalization*);
- a process by which different countries become more and more connected and integrated with each other in various ways, with the end result that all the countries in the world become part of one single global system.

2.1 Clarify the purpose for reading the text before the students start reading, i.e., to confirm existing knowledge and/or to learn something new about globalization.

2.2 After the students have completed the highlighting task, elicit some of the ideas that they found were similar to the ones on their lists, along with some that were not. Obviously, students will have different ideas in each of their lists, so you are not looking for definitive answers here.

Text 6-2 | The shrinking planet

Task 3: Thinking about the topic

To save time, the first three exercises may be done as whole-class activities.

3.1 Clarify the meaning of *shrinking* if necessary (getting smaller). Provide other guidance towards a reasonable answer as necessary.

Possible answers:
- The planet has shrunk as the result of improved communications.
- Goods from other countries are more accessible.

3.2 Encourage students to think about their own experiences and the situation in their own countries. Students may mention other global brands, e.g., *Nike*®, the global impact of the Internet, tourism, etc.

3.3 Ask students to offer suggestions of examples of how globalization might increase differences. Don't worry if they don't come up with very much, the activity is just designed for them to be alert to such differences when they go on to read the text. Avoid the temptation to offer any ideas of your own at this stage.

3.4 This activity previews key vocabulary in the text. There are a number of words and expressions in the box, but it is expected that students will already know some of them. Students check their understanding in pairs or small groups and make suggestions about the likely topic of the text. There is no need to elicit suggestions from them afterwards.

3.5 Get students to match the words and phrases either to the term *differences* or the term *similarities*, or to *convergence* and *divergence* (which links this with later reading texts). Thus, *discontent* = divergence; *common interests* = convergence, etc.

If you feel it would be appropriate to carry out this task as a whole-class task (depending upon the level of the students), the groupings below are given as a suggestion.

Possible answers:

Convergence	Divergence
• cultural convergence • universal links • common interests • similar products • homogenizing effect	• discontent • grievances • alien modern cultures • national culture, history and language • local requirements • customization of products • human peculiarities

Digital technology and *the Internet* do not obviously fit into either column, but should provide a source of debate. This is to be encouraged, as the students will then be developing an engagement with the text. Refer to lines 41–47 of the text for the author's view on these two aspects. Some of the other terms in the box above, e.g., *national culture*, *history and language* may also provoke debate. Students can be encouraged to argue for or against the categorization of any of the terms.

Task 4: Recalling the text from memory

4.1 Deal with the questions on pages 58–59 about the subheading **before** the students go on to read the text.

Answers:
a) The function of the subheading is to expand on the title and therefore give the reader a clearer idea about the contents of the text.
b) The contrast suggested is that despite the effects of globalization, cultural differences have not disappeared.

4.2 **Answer:**
Any differences which are clearly identified in the text are concentrated between lines 35–50. The only specific example is with reference to Muslims; the reference to the Chinese and Scottish is quite general and may need some explaining. When the students have finished reading, move on quickly to Ex 4.3 (recall task).

4.3 Students can either work in pairs or in small groups, with a 'secretary' compiling the recall summary using ideas from group members. They can use the words and expressions they worked with earlier to help them.

Explain to the students that the purpose of recalling the text is to help them to consolidate their understanding. By working together on the recall activity, they can teach each other and fill gaps in their understanding.

4.4 Groups check the text for omissions/inaccuracies. This activity is intended to reinforce their understanding, as well as to provide a purpose for their second reading of the text.

Task 5: Checking the text for details

Get students to highlight, where possible, the first four words of the sentences that give them the answers (or part-sentence in the case of long sentences, such as in paragraph 2). Statement e) may cause a problem, but will encourage students to look carefully at the text.

Answers:
Yes = a), d), h) and i)
No = b), g) and j) *g) is debatable and again should provoke discussion
Not given = c), e) and f)

Task 6: Making use of the text content

6.1 Stress that the focus of this activity is to find out what differences persist among the whole group. You may find it useful to arrange the class in larger groups than normal and then have a general discussion to finish off. Make sure that all the students make a note of significant similarities and differences.

You may need to identify specific issues before the students decide what their attitudes are, e.g., for 'Foreign goods', students might discuss whether it is good for people to have a wide variety of goods available, given that this puts local people out of a job. Don't allow discussion on this to last more than ten minutes.

6.2 This should work most effectively as a whole-class activity.

Either the majority of students have the same attitude about some or all of the categories, **or** the majority of students have a different attitude about some or all of the categories.

In either case, students may be able to come to a general conclusion about the impact of globalization on their own reading class group.

Display the conclusion reached by the students after the class discussion on the board or an OHP.

Task 7: Reading for a purpose

It may be necessary to define the term *social diversity*, e.g., *a situation in which a community of people (or society) has many different elements*.

There are two parts to this summarizing task, and it is important that students spend most of their time on completing the second part, i.e., finding evidence in the text to support their answer. It may be advisable to negotiate a summary for the first part, i.e., the extent to which students agree or disagree with the statement. This could be done as a whole-class activity (on the board) or by individual groups.

Every section of the unit is probably relevant to the question. It is important to remind students to refer back to the previous two sections, *Introduction* and *The shrinking planet*, as well as the texts that follow.

Among other purposes, the task is intended to encourage students to make use of the titles and subtitles, as well as the summaries in the margin or boxes (which might be regarded as abstracts). A heading such as *The sharing of sovereignty* should help students to realize that there is evidence in the texts to support the argument that there *is* social convergence, despite the compelling evidence also supplied to the contrary.

7.1 A number of ideas may occur to students.

Possible answers:
- looking at headings/subheadings/notes;
- keeping the focus task, i.e., the reason for reading, firmly in mind;
- reading the first and last paragraphs of each text as well as the first sentence of each intervening paragraph – or whichever sentence introduces the topic of a paragraph – if one can be identified;
- scanning for key words related to the question; ways of noting relevant information, etc.

7.2 This procedure could be added to the list of ideas above.

7.3 Try to get students to justify their choices orally as they are working on the task.

7.4 Whether students work on this individually or in groups will depend very much on their level and the time available for completing the unit. At higher levels, students can work on this individually, whereas with lower levels, or where time is short, students can work in groups.

Text 6-3 | Economic globalization

Task 8: Asking questions about the text

8.1 The aim of this task is to encourage students to read more carefully by focusing on the content of the text, rather than laboriously deciphering vocabulary on a line-by-line basis. Explain to students that one way of getting a better understanding of the text is by asking questions about it as they read, and looking for the answers. This should also help them to develop summarizing skills.

An important part of this task is for the students to decide how relevant the answers they have found are to answering the question *Has social diversity generally increased as the result of economic globalization?* Students should be told to look at the contents of margin notes, etc., as well as the main text.

Answers:
a) Globalization can cause unemployment.
b) volume of trade and foreign capital investment
c) computer programming and banking
d) the WTO (World Trade Organization), the GATT rounds and the European Union
e) cultural differences, domestic regulations, language barriers and 'private collusive behaviour and information asymmetries'. This last item will need to be explained to most students, i.e., secret/conspiratorial actions and non-regular information – the meaning is not entirely clear from the text.
f) erection of trade barriers/protectionism
g) Because it can provide the conditions for sudden exchange rate fluctuations (in margin notes). Students might also mention the competition that leads to corner shops being replaced by supermarkets.
h) The availability or non-availability of goods from other parts of the world.
i) Industrialized countries
j) The widening gap between rich and poor, commercial thinking spreading to all social areas and the eroding of social manners and other values because of consumerism.
k) Larger/more sophisticated companies are aware of their social responsibilities and the importance of sustainability.

8.2/8.3 This is an important part of the task. Students need to clarify which of the information they have just discovered will be valuable for answering the overall question.

Task 9: Identifying key information in the text

Check that students refer to the paragraphs of the main text only, i.e., not the notes.

Answers:
A3, B7, C4, D1, E5, F8, G2, H6

Task 10: Preparing to complete the Focus task

This task encourages students to review the work they have done so far in this unit. As a result, the list they started in Ex 7.4 should now have been revised.

At this point, three texts are available for exploitation: *Community & conflict*; *The sharing of sovereignty*; *Converging or diverging?* For the first of these texts, *Community & conflict*, some specific tasks are provided. The other two texts, *The sharing of sovereignty* and *Converging or diverging?*, are to be exploited as the students consider appropriate, in order to answer the overall question as follows:

Has social diversity generally increased as the result of economic globalization?

Alternatively, if time is a problem or it is felt that students are not yet ready for longer periods of individual reading, the class could be divided into three groups to carry out a jigsaw-reading task:
Group 1 dealing with *Community & conflict*;
Group 2 with *The sharing of sovereignty*;
Group 3 with *Converging or diverging?*

After working on their particular text, each group should produce a list of points that they consider relevant to the summarizing task, and which the other groups will read for homework or in class (as appropriate). Each group will also need to refer to the two texts they haven't read in order to assess the appropriacy of the summaries provided by the other two groups. Afterwards, students should produce a two-paragraph summary of the main ideas they would use to complete the Focus task as an assignment for a university lecturer.

To answer the question, students should use any evidence they can find in the texts in this unit. They may also make use of their own experience and the experience of other members of their group. Their answer should be quite short – no longer than two paragraphs.*

* If you decide to take this approach, then you should ignore the remaining teacher's notes for this unit.

Text 6-4 | Community & conflict

Task 11: Thinking about the topic

11.1 Answers:
One possibility is that the text will discuss ways that globalization brings people together and also how it divides them.

11.2 Answers:
Causes of conflict include:
1. migration (brought on by a range of possible causes, e.g., natural disaster, over-population, political oppression);
2. religion;
3. traditional, deep-seated problems between nations or groups of people;
4. border disputes;
5. jealousy;
6. economic reasons.

11.3 Answers:
The contrast between the typical idea of the village as a close-knit 'community' and the reality of 'inequality' brought about by the widening gap between rich and poor – the result of economic globalization.

Task 12: Developing understanding of the text

12.1 Answers:
Citizens of the global village are typically (from the text):
- more prosperous;
- part of a new minority group;
- endorsing the universal brotherhood of man;
- multi-ethnic;
- multi-cultural;
- urbanized;
- privileged;
- technology-literate;
- employed in a service industry.

Task 13: Identifying relevant information for the Focus task

13.1 Answers:
Causes of conflict mentioned in the text are:
- loss of jobs;
- national grievances directed against 'foreigners';
- the proliferation of nationalist militia groups;
- fringe groups and 'eccentric' individuals;
- groups illegally making use of CMC;
- the inability to 'enforce national law on the global village'.

13.3 Again, this is an important part of the task. Students need to clarify which parts of the information they have just discovered will be valuable for answering the overall question.

Task 14: Completing an assignment

This is the final stage in the whole process. Students need to review all the information they have discovered in earlier tasks that seems relevant to the overall question, and should use this as the basis for their final two-paragraph answer. The remaining two texts are also available for students to exploit in search of more relevant points.

At the answer-writing stage, it may be sufficient for medium- to high-level students to work through this task individually without teacher direction, but with the teacher monitoring and intervening where necessary. You can take in their answers and return them later with comments on how well the question has been answered, given the information available.

With a lower-level group, you may find it more appropriate to have students preparing their answers in small groups or pairs. They can then talk about their answers with other groups/pairs, and you can finish by eliciting possible answers that seem justified by reference to the information available. Outlined on the following pages (69–72) are some key points from each of the texts that might be used to complete the summary task. Each text is dealt with on a separate page for photocopying purposes, in case you want to display the information on an OHP or distribute handouts.

Unit summary

It is particularly important that the students discuss these activities among themselves to gain the maximum benefit.

3   Answers:
relevant, support, experience, evidence

Web resources

BBC Learning English: Insight plus
A programme that looks at and explains key global issues to learners of English. Students can download an audio interview (or read the script) for episode 1 about the pros and cons of globalization. http://www.bbc.co.uk/worldservice/learningenglish/webcast/tae_insight_archive.shtml

Cuesta College
This site suggests strategies to strengthen comprehension skills and help students read longer texts and books. It goes into some detail on the topics of inferring and identifying fact and opinion. http://academic.cuesta.edu/acasupp/AS/310.HTM

Photocopiable handout

Has social diversity generally increased as the result of economic globalization?

Introduction
(Pages 42–43 in the Source Book)

Factors that may be considered relevant to social diversity
- Buying habits are determined by culture as much as income.
- Selling methods, local specifications and advertising appeal are 'localized, not globalized'.
- Regional financial crises (e.g., in Asia) may cause resistance to the idea of economic globalization.

Factors that may be considered relevant to social convergence
- The virtual economy (relating to the financial world) – screen-based economy (but this might also cause suspicion among nations – particularly the poorer nations towards the richer).

The shrinking planet
(Pages 44–45 in the Source Book)

Factors that may be considered relevant to social diversity
- Use of the Internet by 'aboriginal groups' to air their grievances (but this could be interpreted as a converging factor within the aboriginal groups and between the aboriginal groups and their sympathizers).
- Line 35 '… universal links may be more superficial than they seem …'.
- The impact of Islamic and Chinese culture works against the forces of globalization.
- Individuality can stand in the way of globalization (lines 37–40).
- The impact of the 'easy customization of products'.
- The rise of digital technology reduces the impact of the global media.

Factors that may be considered relevant to social convergence
- The suggestion in the text that national heritage and globalization can survive side-by-side, e.g., the 'proud Scotsman' = 'good European'.

Economic globalization
(Pages 45–47 in the Source Book)

Factors that may be considered relevant to social diversity
* The increasing gap between the richer and poorer nations.
* The widening gap between wealthy and poor individuals (marginalization of the poor).

Factors that may be considered relevant to social convergence
* The dramatic increase in the volume of trade.
* The dissolving of trading barriers.
* The rise of the great multi-national corporations.

Community & conflict
(Pages 48–50 in the Source Book)

Factors that may be considered relevant to social diversity
* Citizens of the global village privileged compared with the international poor.
* Localized conflict replacing global war. (NB: Is this simply one form of warfare replacing another?)
* The emergence of nationalist 'fringe' groups.
* The increasing income gap.
* Urbanization (may cause diversity – not clear from the text).
* Globalization can lead to unemployment, which in turn can lead to a reaction against foreign labour.
* Resistance to cultural convergence brought about by the forces of globalization, leading to retaliation from groups such as the Zapatistas.

Factors that may be considered relevant to social convergence
* The unifying force of teenage culture.
* The unifying force of sport (although this can also cause diversity).
* The rise of multi-cultural societies (made possible through urbanization, which in this instance can lead to convergence).
* Modern technological developments may help to erode local culture (as other commodities did in the past), thus diminishing cultural diversity (but see point above re: Zapatistas).

The sharing of sovereignty
(Pages 50–52 in the Source Book)

Photocopiable

Factors that may be considered relevant to social diversity
- There are no obvious sections in the text that are relevant to the belief that economic globalization causes social diversity. The title *The sharing of sovereignty* in itself implies convergence rather than diversity.

Factors that may be considered relevant to social convergence
- The gradual emergence of a cooperative global system (replacing the nation state), as seen by the growth of international organizations.
- The United Nations. (NB: The relevance of the UN in terms of economic globalization is not clearly stated in the text.)
- The development of the European Union.
- The development of free trade areas.
- The role of the US in joining the World Trade Organization, but **opposing** the terms of the Ottawa treaty.

Converging or diverging?
(Pages 53–55 in the Source Book)

Factors that may be considered relevant to social diversity
- Globalization has increased the gap between rich and poor (in fact, a traditional situation is only being exacerbated).
- In the section *The excluded society*, there is reference to the gap between rich and poor (but there is an inferred convergence between rich and rich).
- Economic benefits of tourism only conceal increasing social tensions. (NB: See reference to 'chaotic diversity' in the notes under *Cultural invasions.*)
- The advent of multi-channel broadcasting may neutralize the impact of global broadcasting.

Factors that may be considered relevant to social convergence
- The Japanese model for demonstrating how economic recovery can be achieved '… by adapting western-style institutions and economic management'.
- The growing idea that free markets + strict monetary discipline = better living standards.
- The growing acceptance of the World Bank concept of 'private enterprise' instead of 'public service'.
- Countries (and cultures) that traditionally resisted globalization are gradually adapting to it.
- The spread of international tourism (but this can also cause diversity).

The new linguistic order

This unit will help students:
- read an article on 'the new linguistic order' and use it to complete an assignment;
- practise making use of a specific text to support their ideas;
- develop the skills they have learnt so far on this reading course.

Unit 7 adopts a 'deep-end' approach. The aim is to simulate as closely as possible the type of reading that students are typically expected to carry out in an academic situation.

The aim should be considered as the successful completion of the extended paragraph-writing task. However, depending on level and varying ability within the group, scaffolding is provided at the end of these teacher's guidelines for remedial or consolidation work with individuals. It is important to stress that students should be encouraged to read as extensively as possible in order to complete the writing task. The scaffolding that is provided is intended for the teacher's file, only to be taken out when a student (or students) are clearly failing to make headway with the text.

At the same time, active monitoring of students' notes should ensure that the class as a whole is picking out the relevant details. For this reason, the main points that students should be noting in relation to the assignment are listed in the guidelines. The very nature of the 'top-down' approach to reading means that students will inevitably carry out the work at varying rates, but it is essential to encourage all students to complete the work as quickly as possible in order to develop the ability to handle extensive and often dense texts.

Task 1: Deciding how to read a text

Possible answers:
- Basically, students should consider the following: *What? Why? When? How? How much?* and *How often?* to read. Try writing these questions on the board as a springboard for group or whole-class discussion.
- Students may decide that they should read the article through before they make notes. Encourage them to *read for gist* (general understanding), possibly marking areas of the text where understanding has broken down for closer study at a later stage.
- Students need to *read selectively*, i.e., some parts of the text are more relevant and therefore require closer attention. Encourage students to avoid 'pernicious word-for-word deciphering' at all opportunities. This simply makes reading laborious and students, who may later be confronted with literally hundreds of pages of reading per week when they begin or continue their academic studies, will have to learn to read selectively if they are going to be able to cope.
- Students should also be encouraged to consider their *reading purpose* (in this case, to carry out an assignment about language developments in Zambia). This will help to encourage selective reading.
- Students should also consider *how to make notes*. Should they, in fact, mark parts of the text that seem relevant and then go back and make notes when the reading is finished, or should they make notes as they are writing? They may decide to read the text in sections and make notes at the end of each section.
- Students might decide to *text-map* – in other words, read through to the end of the text and then note what they have remembered, before going back to supplement these notes. Given the length of the text, this is unlikely to be successful, although it could be attempted in sections after the initial reading. This may work with sections of text, and certain tasks in this book encourage the *recall method* as a way of supplementing understanding.
- Students should be encouraged to decide *how to tackle unknown vocabulary*. For example, their reading will be neither fast nor efficient if they make constant reference to a dictionary at

this stage, and they will make the reading task hard work. However, the students will need to develop their *sight vocabulary* in order to develop their reading fluency.

One method that could be encouraged is to tell students to *limit the number of words* they look up, e.g., no more than three per page or five per page. For any other words they don't know and want to know, they could mark them in pencil and then look up when they've finished reading the whole text.

Alternatively, students could approach vocabulary in the way outlined in the introductory unit (Task 5: Dealing with unknown vocabulary – Course Book pages 15–16). Adapted from Day, R.R., & Bamford, J. (1998). *Extensive reading in the language classroom*, Cambridge: CUP.

Task 2: Reading an introductory case study

2.1 **Possible answers:**
Key points that might be mentioned include:
- English is the official language.
- The majority of adults can use English.
- English is a lingua franca.
- It is vital for Zambia to have an official language.
- Multilingualism exists.
- There are a large number of local languages.
- Zambia's neighbours have a variety of official languages (i.e., not all English).

2.2 Direct discussion around other issues, e.g., the significance of other lingua francas existing on Zambia's borders, could lead to the idea of 'language conflicts'. Also, discussion of how local languages overlap Zambia's borders (regionalization) could be covered. The advantages of local languages over a lingua franca could also be discussed, e.g., they are a means of disseminating news and information; providing education, etc., in more remote, inaccessible regions; they are a 'natural' form of communication.

Students may feel that there will be a revival of local languages that could challenge the position of English. The aim here should be simply to raise awareness. It is probably best not to let discussion go on too long.

2.3 This is a further awareness-raising activity meant to encourage the students to engage with the text (personalization). Terms such as 'multilingual' are explained in the following task (Text 7-1, Task 3) and should require no more than an oral explanation at this stage. Students must, of course, be encouraged to justify their order.

Text 7-1 The new linguistic order

2.4 Refer back to Task 1 (page 73) with reference to note-taking. Explain to students that as they read the text they need to make notes that are relevant to the Focus task. Tell them that they will be told when to read and make notes.

Task 3: Understanding subject-specific vocabulary

3.1 As explained in the Course Book (page 69), it is normal for a reader to have a *working vocabulary* derived from the classroom, prior knowledge, earlier reading, handouts, etc. In other words, *subject-specific vocabulary*. For this reason, key words are supplied at this point, to be matched to the appropriate definitions (mostly taken from the *Longman dictionary of applied linguistics* by Richards, Platt & Weber). Encourage students to scan paragraphs A–C, locate the words and attempt to work out the meaning from context before using a dictionary.

Answers:
a) 4   b) 3   c) 5   d)1   e) 2

3.2 **Answers:**
1h)   2f)   3c)   4a)   5b)   6j)   7d)   8e)   9i)   10g)

Task 4: Predicting content to help understanding

4.1 The key points in the opening three paragraphs are:
- The number of English-language 'users' far outweighs the number of native-speakers.
- English has a wide-ranging role in, for example, diplomacy, air-traffic control, business, industry, banking (but note efforts within the EU to stem the flow).
- The future impact of English may be restricted, its use may even decrease. Suggested reasons include historical precedents, elitism and competition via regionalization and localization.

4.2 In journal articles, there is usually no contents page for the students to refer to, and in this case there is no abstract either. At this point, the students are encouraged to predict the contents of the text based on their understanding of the introductory paragraphs (A–C). It is suggested that students tackle reading actively by framing questions in their mind regarding the likely contents and possible relevance of the article.

The idea behind getting the students to devise a list of possible contents is two-fold. Firstly, it is a simple consciousness-raising exercise. Secondly, it will encourage students to list points in a concise and organized manner. The way this should be introduced is left to the discretion of the individual teacher, although one way could be as follows:

Elicit possible answers to the example question:
Why has English become a global language?

Then elicit and write up, e.g., *trade*. Elicit two more reasons, e.g., *colonization, technology*. Tell the class: *These are three possible reasons. Can you organize them more appropriately and continue the possible list of contents?* The order, for example, might be chronological or in terms of importance.

Elicit another general question about the future of English as a global language: *Will English continue to be a global language in the future?*

If the answer is 'no', tell the students:
Possible reasons for the decline of English as a global language in the 21ˢᵗ century:
- Rise of a new 'global' language
- Developments in technology

Tell the students: *Quickly continue the list. Keep the reasons as brief and succinct as possible.*

If the answer to the question *Will English continue to be a global language in the future?* is 'yes', students should list reasons.

Note: This exercise should take no more than 15 minutes and may not be appropriate for a more advanced group.

Questions such as the ones below may be used to provide scaffolding for students. However, bear in mind that the aim is for students to develop the ability to question the text actively *without* being given such prompts, i.e., to form their own questions before or during reading. In this way, students are being encouraged to focus on meaning rather than language, and thereby to develop a manageable approach to extensive reading.

Once some or all of these questions have been displayed and/or elicited, students should be encouraged to form similar questions of their own as they continue reading.

Possible questions:
- Why has English become such an important language in countries like Zambia?
- What other languages might compete with English for global status?
- Do you think a regional language might replace English?
- What factors may influence the spread of a particular language?
- Will English continue to be an elitist language?
- Will local languages continue to survive in countries like Zambia?

Task 5: Selecting relevant information from the text

Remind students that they are reading in order to carry out an *assignment*. As they read (depending on level), check that students are noting some or all of the points that are listed below.

Teachers may decide with more advanced groups to photocopy the listed points on pages 78–81 for students to compare with their own points and for group/class discussion.

The key points selected on the following pages are by no means exclusive, but they should act as a checklist to ensure that students note-taking is on the right track. Students should begin to realize that this section is providing powerful reasons for the decline of English as a global 'force'.

If a student is clearly failing to pick out the relevant key points, they should be given the tasks that follow (pages 82–84) as further help. Students who have completed their note-taking may still want to complete these tasks to consolidate their understanding.

Supplementary task 1
You may decide to use the matching task on page 82 to check understanding and/or as a skimming exercise.

Answers:
A8) B5) C2) D3) E9) F4) G1) H10) I6) J7)

Supplementary task 2
Students read the short summaries on page 83 and match each one with one of the paragraphs K–N in the text.

Answers:
K4) L1) M3) N2)

Supplementary task 3
Students match the short summaries on pages 84–85 with the appropriate paragraphs in the text.

Answers:
O2) P7) Q1) R10) S9) T5) U6) V4) W8) X3)

Task 6: Fulfilling your reading purpose

It is important that a writing task should be carried out at the end of this unit to reinforce the point that the students' reading at this level is, in fact, task (or assignment) driven. However, it is mainly content that should be assessed (the language and other features of effective writing being the main preserves of other classes). The key points, together with the summaries provided above for the purposes of monitoring and scaffolding, can also be used to assess the content of the students' responses to the tasks. Students should not be expected to write more than two or three paragraphs (an extended summary), which should focus on main points and show their ability to differentiate between main and supporting ideas.

Feedback should direct students back to appropriate areas of the text to consolidate their understanding.

Unit summary

3   **Possible answers:**
   a) Look at displayed information; read the heading and subheadings; make predictions; write some questions.
   b) Select what you think is most relevant; highlight key points.
   c) Recall key points; write down what you remember in note form.

Web resources

Learners of the future
An article by David Graddol which examines the future of English, and considers issues such as how language learning will change and whether students will learn the same way in the future.
http://www.bbc.co.uk/worldservice/learningenglish/radio/specials/1720_ten_years/page9.shtml

Love thy neighbour's language

[Paragraphs D–J]

Key points:

- Colonization promoted spread of English. [para D]

- Relationship between English and globalization: 'contributor to and consequence of'. [para E]

- English 'inextricably' linked to class, sex, age and status. [para F]

- Internationally, English knowledge is 'superficial'. [para F]

- Regionalization relevant to needs of wide range of local populations, e.g., Swahili rather than English (E. Africa); Hausa (W. Africa); Arabic, Woloff and Pidgin in parts of West Africa. [para G]

- Regional languages likely to increase in importance because of growing influence of filmmakers, missionaries, business, etc. [para G and para J]

- Impact of increased regional communication leading to spread of regional languages. [para G]

- Efforts by government and religious organizations to promote other languages. [para I]

- Regional languages promoted for a number of facilitating roles, e.g., dissemination of knowledge. [para J]

Photocopiable

Home is where the tongue is

[Paragraphs K–N]

Key points:

- Resistance/revival of local languages to both globalization and regionalization. [para K]

- Instinctive loyalty to local languages (mark of authenticity). [para L]

- Authenticity and local languages – different strands combining against threat of global or regional languages. [para L]

- Large number of standardized languages (1,200) suggests likelihood of survival of local languages. [para M]

- Local languages serve different functions, e.g., educational/political/social, e.g., intimate language use on Internet. [para M]

- Impact of state-sponsored and voluntary organizations in response to threat of global English. [para M]

- Various campaigns, e.g., language immersion. [para M]

- Pragmatic value of local languages and examples suggesting need for multiliteracy. [para N]

Looking ahead

[Paragraphs O–X]

Key points:

- Size of language should not prevent revival of local languages. [para O]

- Multilingualism can exist if language use is dependent on different functions (or vice versa). [para P]

- English often used as 'sometime' language. [para P]

- Language conflicts occur where languages overlap functions. [para Q]

- Political motives can bring about language conflict, e.g., in Russia. [para Q]

- Language conflicts usually occur between regional and local languages, but sometimes between global and national languages, e.g., English versus French. [para R]

- French response to language of globalization = official neologisms. [para R]

- 'Power' languages feel threatened by minority languages and vice versa. [para S]

- Linguistic globalization, regionalization and localization occurring simultaneously, but at different rates and with differing impact and examples. [para T]

- Informal oral regional and local impact on English – idiosyncratic – learners of English being taught by second-language speakers, etc. [para U]

- Linguistic democracy doesn't really exist – despite efforts by governments to protect concept of 'right of language choice'. [para V]

- Local languages therefore threatened by global and regional languages. [para V]

- English may be increasingly resented and opposed by stronger language communities. [para W]

- English may become increasingly elitist. [para W]

- In all aspects, English may become less indispensable as technology develops. [para W]

- If use of English declines, the forces that brought about its global status may not necessarily lose their own current status. [para X]

Supplementary task 1: Matching task for paragraphs A–J

Here are some short summaries. Each one goes with one of the paragraphs [A–J], but they are not in the correct order. Can you put them in the correct sequence?

1) Although many Africans are multilingual, they often don't speak English because it is less useful to them than the languages they do speak.

2) Despite the strong position of English in the world, the long-term trend may be for it to become less important.

3) English first became internationally important because of England's historical role in the world.

4) Generally, only certain types of people are effective users of English as a foreign language. The situation is not likely to change in the future.

5) Important international uses of English mean that people who speak it are often in a better position than those who don't.

6) One reason why regional languages are becoming more important is that various government and religious organizations throughout the world are encouraging their use.

7) Regional languages will become increasingly important as a way of facilitating communication in places where local languages are spoken.

8) The use of English is growing throughout the world in an uncontrolled fashion.

9) There are a number of reasons why English is currently increasing in international importance. Some of them are less obvious than others.

10) The demand for regional languages is increasing rapidly.

A	B	C	D	E	F	G	H	I	J
8)									

Supplementary task 2: Matching task for paragraphs K–N

Here are some short summaries. Each one goes with one of the paragraphs [K–N], but they are not in the correct order. Can you put them in the correct sequence?

1) Local languages provide an attachment with the cultural background of the people who speak them. As a result, growing efforts will be made to preserve them.
2) Apart from personal preference, the practical uses that local languages can be put to suggest that they can survive alongside more widespread languages.
3) Strong efforts are being made to raise the status of, and thus preserve, local languages. This is being achieved through the efforts of certain agencies to promote the functional uses of such languages.
4) The spread of globalization will inadvertently develop a growing need to preserve things that have a more intimate value.

K	L	M	N
4)			

Supplementary task 3: Matching task for paragraphs O–X

Match the following short summaries with the appropriate paragraphs in the text.

1) Political force can be the cause of dissent within or between language communities, especially if a language is forced on a community.

2) The number of speakers of a language should not necessarily determine whether that language will survive or not.

3) The use of English will probably become less necessary as technology develops even further, but the positive features associated with the spread of English may survive, even if the language itself declines.

4) Very often, language speakers are not really given the opportunity to speak the language of their choice, despite official claims that they have this right.

5) The effects of global, regional and local languages are occurring at the same time in various parts of the world, but at different rates and with varying impact.

6) English is being affected by regional variation, especially in an informal context, such as everyday conversations.

7) In many countries, different languages are used for different purposes, which suggests that the people of certain countries must raise their literacy level in more than one language.

8) There are reasons to suggest that English will gradually become less popular and that it will exist mainly as the language of an elite minority.

9) There are different opinions about whether minority languages cause a threat to majority languages or whether it is the majority language that is the main threat.

10) When tension develops between a major national language and a global language, such as English, official efforts are sometimes made to invent new words to replace words from the global language that are beginning to appear in the national language.

O	P	Q	R	S	T	U	V	W	X
2)									